SCALE, INNOVATION, MERGER AND MONOPOLY

SCALE, INNOVATION, MERGER AND MONOPOLY

An Introduction to Industrial Economics

by HARRY TOWNSEND

PERGAMON PRESS

OXFORD · LONDON · EDINBURGH · NEW YORK
TORONTO · SYDNEY · PARIS · BRAUNSCHWEIG

PERGAMON PRESS LTD.
Headington Hill Hall, Oxford
4 & 5 Fitzroy Square, London W.1
PERGAMON PRESS (SCOTLAND) LTD.
2 & 3 Teviot Place, Edinburgh 1
PERGAMON PRESS INC.
44–01 21st Street, Long Island City, New York 11101
PERGAMON OF CANADA LTD.
207 Queen's Quay West, Toronto 1
PERGAMON PRESS (AUST.) PTY. LTD.
19a Boundary Street, Rushcutters Bay, N.S.W. 2011
PERGAMON PRESS S.A.R.L.
24 rue des Écoles, Paris 5e
VIEWEG & SOHN GmbH
Burgplatz 1, Braunschweig

First edition 1968
Library of Congress Catalog Card No. 68–24069

Printed in Great Britain by A. Wheaton & Co., Exeter

08 012941 2 (flexicover)
08 012942 0 (hard cover)

CONTENTS

LIST OF FIGURES

LIST OF TABLES

PREFACE

THIS book is addressed to readers in the early stages of undergraduate study of economics and to those preparing for professional examinations in accounting and banking. Participants in courses of management studies may find some instruction in an economist's-eye-view of industry. One always hopes that lots of other readers will be attracted in addition to those intended. The topics discussed are of practical as well as academic importance.

It is sometimes difficult to decide what to include and what to leave out of an introductory textbook. There has been no such problem here. I have included things that interest me, and excluded the rest. My hope is that my interests have some coherence and that interesting writing makes enjoyable reading. The approach is that of an economist using economic theory to provide the main conceptual framework, but I have not scrupled to borrow bits of political science, sociology and social psychology when they seemed useful.

Bold dots are used instead of numbers to give emphasis without priority to points, and to emphasise separate parts of the chapter summaries. In Chapter 8, this is carried one stage further with a single dot against disadvantages and double dots against advantages.

I am grateful to K. J. W. Alexander, E. W. Benson, R. G. Gould, K. Klappholz, B. McCormich and B. S. Yamey for reading and commenting on parts of the manuscript. They are none of them to blame for the text which remains. I am also grateful to the London School of Economics for providing secretarial assistance.

London School of Economics H. T.
November 1967

PART ONE

Scale and Efficiency

INTRODUCTION

ECONOMIES of scale deserve our attention because they are associated with important economic policies, give rise to large economic problems, and help to explain features of industrial organisation.

The search for economies of scale played a part in the most dramatic development of post-war years, the setting up of the European Economic Community. In Britain industries have been nationalised and encouraged to merge. The Industrial Reorganisation Corporation has been provided with £150 million to promote amalgamations by loans from public funds.

There are problems as well as opportunities. Companies may be so big that they monopolise markets. This problem was first met in the "natural monopolies", such as gas, water and electricity supply and rail transport, where public utility undertakings were regulated and later nationalised. In the private sector there is need to distinguish the firm that dominates because it sells more cheaply from the firm that dominates and exploits. Even when monopoly is not in question, big business may still be a problem simply because of its size. The market keeps small businessmen in check, but the self-elected oligarchs at the head of large corporations are less circumscribed as they wield their power.

Beyond policies and problems are the straightforward questions of understanding. Why is it less costly to assemble 100 planes instead of 50? Why is it more efficient to refine 10 million tons of oil a year rather than 1 million? Why are firms the size they are? Why is research and development undertaken only in a narrow sector of the economy? What is automation? Is it always a boon? Why do firms merge? Why are processes sometimes specialised and sometimes integrated within one organisation? How is the survival of small firms explained? These are some of the questions we attempt to answer in this part.

The economies of large outputs and merits of large organisations are considered first. This leads to a discussion of technological advance, research and development and automation, where large organisations have played the main part. Next the formation of large companies by merger is considered, and, finally, the survival of small firms is examined.

Chapter 1

ECONOMIES OF LARGE-SCALE PRODUCTION

COSTS per unit of output may be reduced for technological reasons as a result of producing a large output rather than a small one. They may also be reduced, for other reasons, by producing in a large organisation, which administers many lines of production, rather than in a small organisation. This distinction is worth making because technology may present opportunities for savings in unit-costs as output expands, but it is not a source of cost increases as output expands further: with organisation there may be diseconomies as well as economies. Technological conditions may be such that there is a least-cost scale of production, but there is no technological reason why costs should rise beyond this scale. The least-cost plant may be repeated as many times as is necessary (Fig. 1).

This chapter is only concerned with technological economies associated with large outputs. Large organisations are considered in Chapter 2. Technology varies, of course, from industry to industry, so it is impossible to give a complete account of technological economies. We can, however, point to some of the main sources of such cost savings. Problems of measuring economies of scale are then examined, and the chapter concludes with some indications of typical orders of magnitude.

A large output may refer to a large cumulative total or to a large rate of output. These two are connected. The larger the rate of output per week, the larger will be the cumulative total over time. If 2 aircraft are completed per week the cumulative total in a year will be 104; if the rate of output is 1 per week the cumulative

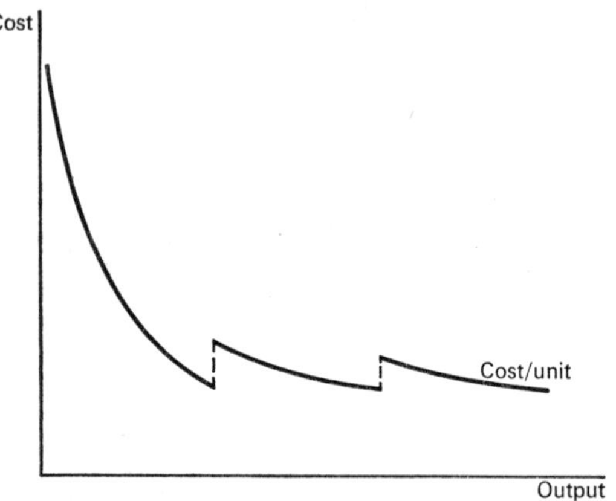

FIG. 1. Technological economies always work in one direction as least-cost plant may be duplicated.

total in a year will be 52. Large cumulative totals of output and large rates of output both give rise to economies.

Economies of large cumulative output: learning

It has long been known that practice makes perfect, but one industrial application of this maxim was only noticed recently in the so-called 80 per cent rule of the U.S. aerospace industry. It was found that every time the cumulative output of an aircraft doubled the cost of production fell to 80 per cent of its previous level. If the cost of producing the 50th aircraft was 100, the cost of producing the 100th would be 80, the cost of the 150th would be 64 and so on.

The fall in cost is the result of learning from previous production. As the cumulative total of output rises the workforce becomes more experienced and adept, fewer errors are made, improvements in processes are seen and introduced. The strength of U.S. aerospace firms stems in part from the long runs for single designs which the American market provides.

Learning does not only apply to the aircraft industry. In the D.S.I.R. National Building Study 29 there is report of an investigation on two large building sites. The man-hours required to carry out various types of building work on blocks of two two-storey semi-detached houses were measured by order of construction. The man-hours needed are shown in Fig. 2.

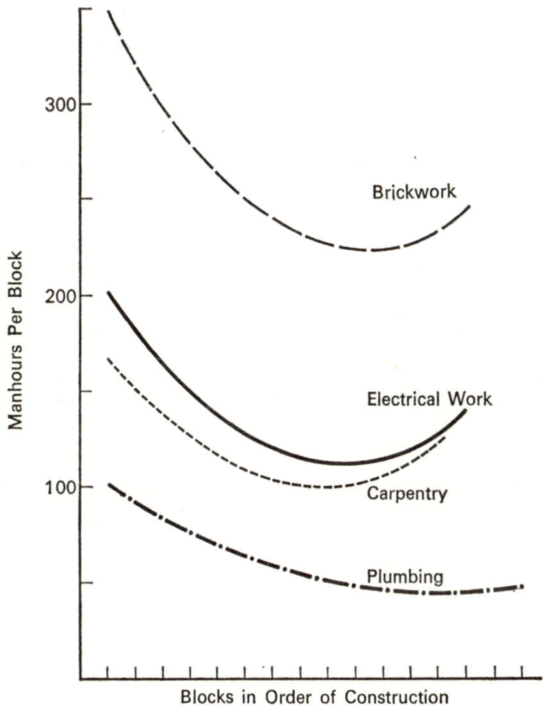

FIG. 2. Improvement curves in building. "Block" denotes two traditional two-storey semi-detached houses. (Source: R. C. Sansom, *Organisation of Building Sites*, London, H.M.S.O., 1959.)

Economies of large rates of output

As the rate of output rises there are four places to look for possible economies of scale:

- Set-up costs may be once-and-for-all.

- Large numbers may provide regularity in place of unpredictability.
- Area–volume relationships may mean that construction costs do not rise in proportion to capacity.
- Machinery may be indivisible, and with given capacity for each item of machinery the least-cost plant will be that producing an output equal to the lowest common multiple of the individual capacities.

Set-up costs. Some costs must be incurred at the start of production but do not need to be repeated as production continues. Simple examples are the fixing of dies in a drop stamp or new rolls in a steel mill. Similar economies of much greater importance may be found.

The cost of designing and developing a new aircraft is much the same whether one aircraft or one hundred are to be produced. As the design and development function becomes more complex, the viable scale of production gets larger. A firm introducing a new aircraft engine may build seven prototypes at a cost of £250,000 each and test them to destruction. It is not surprising that only one aircraft engine manufacturer has survived in Britain and that there should only be two others of note in the non-communist world.

Computers provide another example. In addition to designing and producing the electronic hardware computer firms need to provide software, programmes that customers may use without too much preliminary work of their own. The software for a new computer may cost £5 million. Once this cost has been incurred it does not have to be repeated in order that the same programmes may be offered to new clients.

The same economy may be seen at work in newspapers. Writing and editing the first copy is a similar task whatever the circulation. The larger the circulation the less these costs are per copy. In 1965, the *Daily Mirror* had an average net daily circulation of 5 million copies; the *Sun*, owned by the same publisher, had a circulation of 1·3 million. Editorial costs were 11 per cent of the total costs of the *Mirror* and 24 per cent of those of the *Sun*.

Setting up the presses for printing is also less costly per copy for the large circulation daily. This same economy was neatly illustrated by Pratten and Dean for different-sized prints of a 256-page paperback book (Table 1).

TABLE 1. Printing Costs for Paperbacks (1961).

Printing order (number)	Printing costs (d. per copy)	Paper cost (d. per copy)	Total (d. per copy)	Index
5,000	17·5	3·4	20·9	100
20,000	9·1	3·1	12·2	59
50,000	5·3	3·1	8·4	41
100,000	3·9	3·1	7·0	34

These costs are estimates for a 256-page book.
Source: C. Pratten and R. M. Dean, in collaboration with A. Silberston, *The Economies of Large-scale Production in British Industry*, Cambridge, 1965.

Large numbers. As the sample size of a random variable increases, its variance about the mean decreases. When costs depend upon the variance there is economy in producing on a large scale. In other words, laws of large numbers may be associated with economies of scale.

For example, stocks need to be kept against unexpected demands. As demand grows it becomes more regular and provision for the unexpected can be proportionately smaller. The same applies to maintenance crews. A large aircraft fleet may be kept in repair for less cost per aircraft than a small fleet. Again, joining electricity generating stations by the National Grid enabled larger total demand to be supplied with fewer generating stations than would otherwise have been required. This economy is now pursued further by connections between national grids.

Area–volume relationships. Areas vary with the square of dimensions and volumes with the cube. The surface area of three-dimensional objects does not increase as fast as the volume. When cost depends upon area and output on volume, costs per unit of output fall with increased scale. If it costs £15 to clothe an eight-stone man, it will not cost £30 to clothe one of sixteen stones: twice the cloth and tailoring will not be needed.

The same applies to other containers such as tanks and pipes. Chemical engineers have a "six-tenths rule", that Cost = $(\text{Capacity})^{0.6}$, for the plant they design. Large oil refineries, for example, are less costly to build per unit of refining capacity than small refineries. Similarly, large pipelines are less costly per unit of capacity than small ones, and one super-mammoth oil-tanker is less costly to build than two supertankers of the same total capacity. A tanker of 200,000 tons costs about £5 million, whereas two 100,000-ton tankers would cost about £6·6 million, £3·3 million each.

Indivisibility and the principle of multiples. Two half pencils are as good as one whole one, but two half typewriters are no good at all. The fact that machinery usually has a minimum efficient size lies behind many economies of scale. If output is not sufficient to utilise much of the capacity of a machine, resort must be had to more primitive methods. The lowest unit costs will not be within reach.

Production is seldom achieved with one kind of machine, and so costs per unit fall with output up to the point where all the complementary machinery is being used to capacity. This is at an output equalling the least common multiple of capacities of individual items of plant. It has been estimated that in motor car manufacturing lowest unit costs may be achieved in assembly with a conveyor line handling 100,000 cars per year. In the machine shop, where much more complicated plant is employed such as automatic transfer lines for machining main castings, lowest costs per engine are found with an output of 500,000 engines per year. In the body-pressing shop the huge presses have a capacity of 1 million bodies per year. The minimum optimum scale is, therefore, 1 million cars per year produced with one body-pressing shop, two machine shops and ten assembly lines.[1]

[1] See G. Maxcy and A. Silberston, *The Motor Industry*, London, 1959.

Measuring economies of large outputs

Although it is easy to identify sources of economies of scale, measuring such economies has proved difficult. Five methods have been employed:

- comparison of costs in existing plants;
- comparison of profits in firms of different sizes;
- comparison of output per head in establishments of different sizes;
- identification of the size of plant which survives over time; and
- engineering estimates of costs at alternative levels of output.

Plant comparisons. Comparing costs in existing plants with differing capacities is usually an ambiguous undertaking. Products are seldom identical, costs reflect the age structure of machinery which embodies technical knowledge of the time of its manufacture, and capital costs become subjective estimates when old-fashioned plant, no longer bought and sold on the open market, is involved. This method does, however, have the merit of going to primary sources for information. The next three methods depend upon published data.

Return on capital. The simplest is to compare the return on capital in the published accounts of firms of varying sizes. In the past, the size of firms has been vague because they were not obliged to publish figures of sales turnover and often did not. There is difficulty with the valuation of capital once more, a special problem being the variety of ways in which allowance is made for the irrelevance of historical cost figures in times of inflation. There is the problem that firms generally make a number of products and product-mixes vary, so scale of production is ambiguous. And finally, return on capital reflects other influences, such as managerial efficiency and monopoly power, as well as economies of scale.

Output per head. Instead of published accounts, published statistics may be used. One method is to calculate output per head in establishments of differing size from figures in the Census of Production. This is not satisfactory because a high output per head may result from the use of large amounts of capital per head, and so high *per capita* output may reflect high costs rather than economies of scale. A second difficulty is that the Census classification puts together establishments making different products, e.g. oil refineries of varying complexity, establishments making non-competitive products, e.g. Ford and Rolls-Royce motor cars, and those with differing degrees of vertical integration, e.g. Ford and Rootes.

The survivor technique. The fourth method also suffers from the crudity of the Census classification. It is based on the idea that the sizes of plant which have the minimum costs are the ones which survive over time. This is an attractive approach because it allows all the forces operating within different-sized plants an influence on the outcome; but the fact that technological economies, efficiency of management, suitability to markets, financial strength and established goodwill all play a part means that the survivor technique is not suitable for measuring technological economies alone.

Engineering estimates. Finally, there is the method of obtaining engineering estimates of the likely costs at varying scales of production. These are hypothetical, but they are the figures managements rely on when deciding the scale of plant to install and they have direct reference to economies of large outputs. Engineering estimates were obtained by Bain and by Pratten and Dean for the measures of economies of scale shown in Tables 2 and 3.

The most striking feature of these estimates is the modesty of the economies available. They bulk larger in Britain with a smaller home market than the United States, but, with obvious exceptions such as sheet steel in U.K. and typewriters in U.S.A., the economies of large outputs are not sufficient to explain the size of

TABLE 2. Estimates of Economies of Large Outputs, Selected United States Industries.

Industry	Output of efficient firm as percentage of national market	Cost disadvantage of plant at one-half of fully efficient scale (per cent)
Typewriters	10 to 30	n.i.*
Cigarettes	15 to 20	½ to 1
Steel	2 to 20	n.i.
Soap	8 to 15	3
Cement	2 to 10	5 to 15
Rayon	4 to 6	8
Tyres and tubes	1⅜ to 2¼	1 to 4½
Petroleum refining	1¾	2
Distilled liquor	1¼ to 1¾	1
Canned fruit and vegetables	¼ to ½	n.i.

*n.i. = no information.
Source: J. S. Bain, *Barriers to New Competition*, Cambridge, Mass., 1956.

TABLE 3. Minimum Optimum Size of Plant and Industry Output, Selected British Industries.

Industry	Size of plant	Percentage of total U.K. capacity in 1964
Book printing	300–400 employees	1–2
Footwear	4800 pairs per day	1–2
Bulk steel production	2m. tons/year	7
Sheet steel production	3m. tons/year	50
Oil refining	10m. tons/year	17

Source: C. Pratten and R. M. Dean, *op. cit.*

firms. In Table 4 the 20 largest industrial companies outside U.S.A., measured by sales, are listed. For comparison, in 1966, sales of the largest U.S. company, General Motors, amounted to £7239 million, and of the 20th largest U.S. company, Radio Corporation of America, to £913 million. Sales of these dimensions cannot be explained simply by economies of large outputs. In the next chapter we turn to additional economies and diseconomies that are found within large organisations.

TABLE 4. The Largest Industrial Companies outside U.S.A., 1966.

Company	Sales (£m.)
Royal Dutch/Shell	2754
Unilever	1893
British Petroleum	908
Volkswagenwerk	893*
Imperial Chemical Industries	885
National Coal Board	838
Philips' Gloeilampenfabrieken	796
Montecatini Edison	714
Siemens	699*
Nestlé	608
August Thyssen-Hütte	605*
Fiat	600
Daimler-Benz	527*
British Motor	526
Farbwerke Hoechst	520*
Renault	510
Farbenfabriken Bayer	495*
Hitachi	488
Mitsubishi Heavy Industries	453
Fried. Krupp	444*

Source: "The Fortune Directory", *Fortune*, September 1967. Sales exclude taxes except in the case of German companies, where figures include turnover taxes. *Includes turnover taxes. German companies would rank lower if turnover taxes could be excluded.

Summary

- Producing on a large scale may enable lower costs per unit of output to be achieved. There is no technological reason for costs to rise with scale because optimum-sized plants may be duplicated.
- Economies are associated with a large cumulative output because management and workpeople learn on the job.
- Economies may arise with a large rate of output because set-up costs do not need to be repeated, large numbers increase predictability, area–volume relationships make larger constructions cheaper per unit of capacity, and indivisible equipment may be used in the best proportions.
- Economies of large outputs may be measured by comparing costs in existing plants, comparing returns on capital in published accounts, comparing output per head in different-sized establishments, identifying the scale of survivors, and by engineering estimates.
- There is little evidence that economies of large outputs need involve few firms with large market shares.

Reading

C. Pratten and R. M. Dean, *The Economies of Large-scale Production in British Industry*, Cambridge, 1965.

Chapter 2

ECONOMIES AND DISECONOMIES OF LARGE ORGANISATIONS

ECONOMIES of large outputs are matters of fact. In the appropriate technological circumstances they are bound to be enjoyed. Economies and diseconomies of large organisations are not inevitable: the economies have to be worked for and the diseconomies may be avoided. Possible advantages of large organisations are discussed first, followed by the disadvantages. In conclusion some aspects of the growth of organisations are examined.

Advantages of large organisations

A large organisation may gain because it:

- makes the most of managerial skills;
- recruits and promotes able staff;
- spreads risks;
- obtains finance easily; and
- advertises effectively.

Management. Full-time directors of large companies are paid hundreds of pounds per week. This might be taken as an indication that they fix their own salaries; but, on a long view, it must be recognised that they can only continue to write their own salary cheques because they are scarce and productive. It will be seen later that large organisations need good managers. Beyond the need, they provide scope for scarce talent to make its full contribution.

The point was illustrated by the Fleck Report on the organisation of the National Coal Board. At the time of the report the N.C.B. was the largest employer in the Western world, and there were widespread suggestions that the coal industry should be organised in smaller units. Fleck recommended even greater centralisation in order to make the most of the scarce managerial skill available.

Recruitment and promotion. The fact that large organisations provide opportunity for talent means that they have special attraction to young recruits. Newcomers are employed in sufficient number to justify formal training schemes. There are plenty of openings and so it is less difficult to match ability with employment.

These advantages persist. The recruits later provide a large field of candidates for promotion. Internal promotion is good for morale. It is also more efficient than drawing in higher grade employees from outside because firms know far more about their own employees than they can find out about outsiders. Internal promotion is easier the larger the field of candidates from which to choose.

Spreading risks. A similar advantage is found where the choice is of products rather than of people. Large organisations can put their eggs in lots of baskets. Diversification may be carried too far, as is witnessed by firms dropping products and selling subsidiaries; but within sensible limits, generally set by the firm's special area of knowledge, diversification is a source of strength.

A car firm dependent on a single model might have a Model T Ford or it might have a Ford Edsel. Ford Motors could survive the Edsel fiasco because it had developed a range of cars since its Model T days. Spreading risk is especially important in the science-based industries. The costs of innovation may be borne by the profits from established products, and failures do not cripple the entire organisation.

Finance. Less risk means greater availability and lower rates for finance. Large organisations have advantages in both internal and external finance.

A large organisation generates funds in one part that may be put to work in another with the management acting as a particularly well-informed banker. Ploughed-back profits, which are the main source of long-term finance, are more dependable in large firms.

When recourse is had to the capital market, the advantages of large organisations are more marked. They are well known, and existing profits provide cover for new issues. In addition large organisations raise capital in large amounts. This reduces the proportionate burden of issuing costs and it suits the convenience of financial intermediaries. If an insurance company has £1 million to invest each week it does not want to complicate its portfolio with lots of small investments.

Advertising. The advantage of large organisations as advertisers is partly a consequence of their command of large financial resources. Launching a new product on a national scale by advertising often costs £200,000 or more in the first year. The advantage is also a consequence of risk reduction.

Advertising is a peculiarly uncertain process. The wrong people may get the message; for example, it is said that the main readers of car advertisements are existing owners seeking reassurance. If the message is widely received it may be misunderstood. "Put a tiger in your tank" attracted the widest attention, but the slogan was not always associated with the intended brand of petrol. If the message is widely received and understood, it may be forgotten. The retention rates for advertisements usually turn out to be surprisingly low when measured by sample surveys; 4 per cent of the respondents remembering the message would not be unusual. Finally, advertising that is widely received and remembered may not be acted upon. The advertisement of Strand cigarettes by a lonely man on the Thames Embankment, with the slogan "You are never alone with a Strand", proved memorable to lots of people but few bought this brand. With so many uncertainties, advertising calls for the persistent deployment of large resources.

Disadvantages of large organisations

Large organisations may face problems of

- co-ordination,
- control,
- communication, and
- morale.

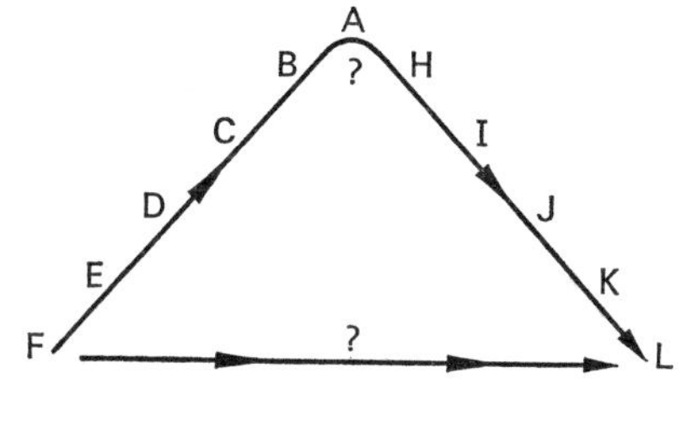

FIG. 3. The problem of co-ordination: should F and L get on with the job by working directly with one another, or should they communicate via the formal chain of command?

Co-ordination. Figure 3 illustrates two wings of a pyramid of management. G is responsible to F who is responsible to E and so on up to A. Similarly M is responsible to L and so on up to A. Suppose F needs to co-ordinate his activities with L. If he deals directly with L, then E, D, C, B, A, H, I, J and K may not know what is going on and fail to take account of the joint activity of F and L higher up the organisation. If F and L follow the formal line of communication, co-ordination will be a time-consuming business wrapped in red tape. This problem is related to the wider one of the span of control.

Span of control. This refers to the number of subordinates a single manager directly co-ordinates. If a manager has two subordinates directly reporting to him the span of control is two, and so on. The larger the organisation the greater the danger that managers at particular stages will accumulate too many responsibilities and disrupt the organisation by attempting to contribute too much.

The number of relationships within a management hierarchy multiply with surprising speed. There are direct single relationships between superior and subordinates (Fig. 4). The number of these equals the number of subordinates.

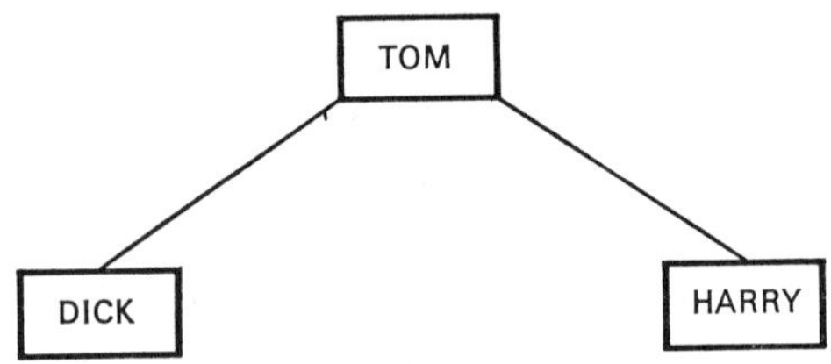

FIG. 4. Direct single relationships (A). In Figs. 4, 5 and 6, n = number of subordinates. A = n.

Secondly, there are cross-relationships between subordinates (Fig. 5). The number possible equals the number of subordinates multiplied by that number minus one.

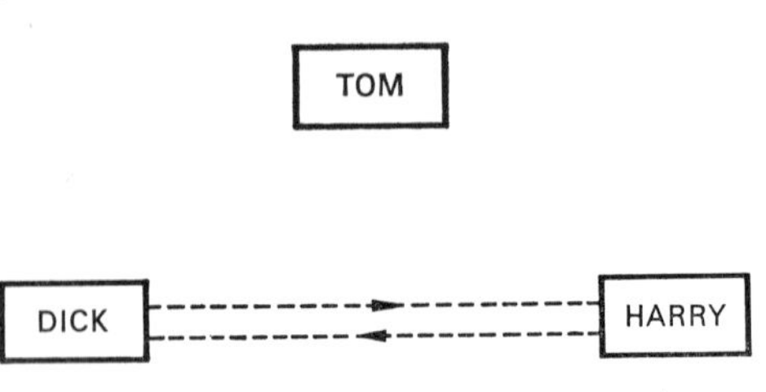

FIG. 5. Cross-relationships (B). B = $n(n - 1)$.

Finally, there are direct-group relationships between superior and subordinates who may be grouped together in many ways

(Fig. 6). The number of these relationships possible increases with the number of subordinates faster than in the other two cases.

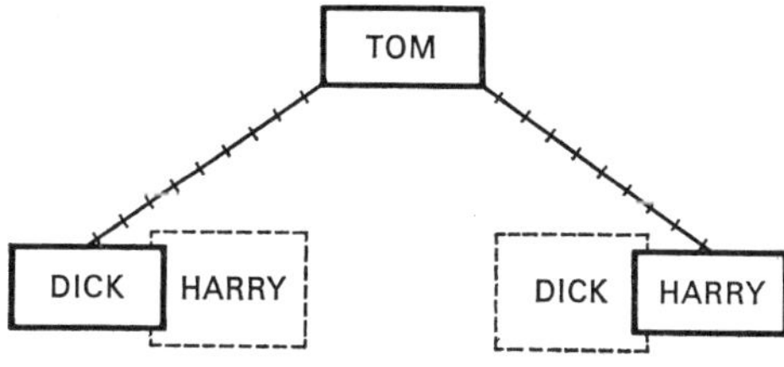

FIG. 6. Direct-group relationships (C). $C = n\left(\frac{2^n}{2} - 1\right)$.

In Table 5 the number of relationships between superior and subordinates are calculated for different spans of control. It will be seen that the number of possible contacts within a hierarchy multiply with great speed as the span of control increases.

TABLE 5. The Increase in Relationships with Increasing Spans of Control.

Number of subordinates (n)	4	5	6 ...	12
Direct-single relationships (A)	4	5	6 ...	12
Cross-relationships (B)	12	20	30 ...	132
Direct-group relationships (C)	28	75	186 ...	24,564
Total (A + B + C)	44	100	222 ...	24,708

(Based on V. A. Graicunas, "Relationship in Organisation", in L. Gulick and L. Urwick (Eds.), *Papers on the Science of Administration*, New York, 1937.)

There is no universally valid rule for the maximum span of control nor for the optimum span. Subordinates like contact with the top and so tend to multiply relationships within a hierarchy. A superior can cope with a larger number of subordinates if their work is independent of one another (for example, the work of branch managers of geographically dispersed plants), or if the administration is largely routine.

A modest span of control does not mean a vast proliferation of layers of management as the size of an organisation grows. In Fig. 7 the number of managers needed to co-ordinate the work of 390,625 operatives is calculated on the assumption that the span of control is 5 at each point in the management. Each manager has 5 subordinates. This assumption is clearly unrealistic. If we give each foreman 20 workers instead of 5, the management would be sufficient for 1,562,500 operatives. In either case a man on the factory floor would only need promoting eight times to rise to be head of the organisation.

Chairman	1
Vice-Chairmen	5
Managing Directors	25
Directors	125
Area Managers	625
Works Managers	3,125
Departmental Managers	15,625
Foremen	78,125
Operatives	390,625

FIG. 7. The progression $1 + 5^1 + 5^2 + 5^3 + \dots 5^{n-1} + 5^n$. A large organisation may be managed with a small span of control. If each foreman had 20 operatives under him there would be 1,562,500 operatives. Soviet communism is arithmetically possible!

Communication. The relationships found with differing spans of control may be regarded as communication networks. In this way they indicate possible problems of communication within large organisations. Communication may be one-way, as when a superior tells a subordinate to do something, or two-way, as when a superior discusses action with a subordinate.

One-way communication is speedy but inaccurate. The classic example of inaccuracy is the army commander who signalled "Send reinforcements I'm going to advance": at headquarters the message was received "Send three and fourpence I'm going to a dance". One-way communication is good for the morale of the transmitter, who says what he wants—but bad for the morale of the receiver, who has simply got to listen. The desire for speed, to get the organisation moving, makes one-way communication very tempting for large organisations.

Two-way communication is more accurate because the receiver can check the message he is receiving; but it is time-consuming. Two-way communication is also better for the morale of receivers.

Morale. Morale is an abiding problem for large organisations. The administrative pyramid is there to be climbed. Early training, education, pay and the prize of status all work to turn people into pyramid climbers. An organisation, therefore, does not simply compete with outside organisations: it is itself the scene of internal competition.

Interpersonal competition within an organisation works best if objective tests of efficiency can be devised, if standards for advancement can be laid down in advance, and if the success of one person can be separated from the failure of others. These requirements are more easily met within the Civil Service than in industry.

Administrative pyramids give rise to other problems. Their very nature implies an unequal distribution of power, with the lower echelons in dependent positions needing the approval of those higher up. It is not difficult for people low down the pyramid to lack any identification of interest with an organisation and to regard it with apathy, if not hostility.

Reviewing the problems of co-ordination, control, communication and morale, large organisations may seem characterised by "inflexibility, unimaginativeness, uniformity, complexity, routine, stratification, delay, dispersion, timidity, unresponsiveness, officiousness, mediocrity and stagnation". It must be remembered that while the problems are real, they are not insoluble. Large organisations get into trouble, but they get out again. They have marked powers of survival. Indeed, they grow.

The growth of organisations

Up to this point we have been considering advantages and disadvantages which may be experienced in organisations of large absolute size. However, firms do not simply exist in big or small sizes. They change and some of them grow. Growth may be internal, when a firm increases the output of existing products or adds new products, or external, when a firm acquires other firms. In this section three aspects of internal growth are examined:

- the absorption and release of managerial resources at different stages in the life of a product;
- the rate of growth; and
- administrative characteristics of growth.

Product cycles. The life of a product may be thought of as consisting of three stages, illustrated in highly stylised form in Fig. 8. In early life, when the rate of output is low, the main people needed are scientists and technologists as techniques of production have yet to be firmly established. Demands upon general management are not great. This changes in the growth stage, the period of

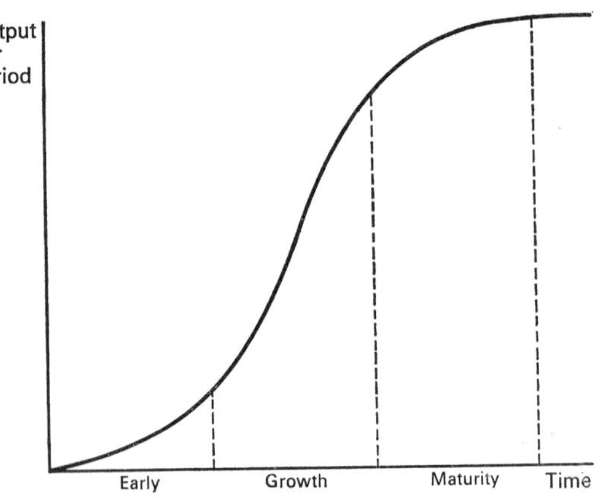

FIG. 8. The product cycle.

the most rapid rate of increase of output. The market for the product must be built up, large capital resources be committed, and competition faced from other producers. The largest demands are made upon management at this time. Later as the product becomes mature its production and sale become more routine and management is released for other tasks.

There may be other stages in the life of a product: stagnation, decline and demise. These are less interesting as there is nothing sacrosanct about such stages. If sales are declining a product may be killed and replaced by another.

The rate of growth. The fact that management is successively absorbed and released at different stages means that as a product reaches maturity manpower becomes available to add new products and to foster further growth. At the end of the early stage, scientists and technologists can move into new fields as general managers take over from them, and the managers may follow later. The rate of growth of the organisation depends upon the pulsation of the product cycle and the extent to which different stages for different products synchronise with one another.

Growth, however, usually requires more scientists, technologists and managers in addition to changing tasks for such people. This puts a second limit on the rate of growth: the speed with which research and development teams and management teams can be built up. Team building calls for help from existing team members and these cannot train newcomers and play their own game at the same time.

Administrative characteristics of growth. Administration does not grow with output to the same extent in all organisations. Administrative needs grow with the size of output, but they also grow with the complexity of output and its geographical dispersion. Growth in the size of output is common to all growing businesses. There is some evidence to suggest that administrative work grows less than in proportion to the number of people performing identical tasks. The administrative work grows more than in proportion to the number of different tasks being performed, and more than in proportion to the number of places at which work is being performed. So long as administrators can keep output growing faster than their own numbers multiply, profitable opportunities for further growth should still appear.

Summary

- Large organisations may be able to produce more cheaply than small ones because they provide scope for first-rate managers, recruit and promote more efficiently, face less risk, obtain finance at lower cost, and advertise more effectively.
- They may run into problems of co-ordinating the work of hierarchies of management; managers may attempt too much and contrive too wide spans of control; communications may be slow and inaccurate; and morale of the workforce may be low.
- There is nothing inevitable about the advantages and disadvantages: the former provide opportunities to grasp, the latter difficulties to overcome.
- Management requirements differ at each stage of the product cycle. As a product reaches maturity the management becomes routine and managers become available for new ventures. With growth additional managers are required, and there is a limit to the speed at which they can be absorbed by existing management teams. Administration grows less than in proportion to the number of people performing identical tasks, and more than in proportion to the number of different tasks and different places of work.

Reading

E. T. Penrose, *The Theory of the Growth of the Firm*, Oxford, 1959.

R. S. Edwards and H. Townsend, *Business Enterprise*, London, 1958.

Chapter 3

RESEARCH AND DEVELOPMENT

ECONOMIES of scale are one source of increases in output per head, improved methods of production are a second. The two are connected in that research and development, devoted to improving methods as well as evolving new products, is an important field in which economies of scale are found. These economies are considered in the first section of this chapter.

In 1964/5, £771·4 million are estimated to have been spent on research and development in the United Kingdom: 2·6 per cent of the Gross National Product. More than 80 per cent of this expenditure was undertaken in capital goods and chemical industries. In the second section the reasons for this concentration are examined. Finally, the problem of determining the adequacy of r. and d. expenditure is discussed.

An appendix is devoted to the economics of the patent system. This system has a special interest because it is an important example of monopoly power being conferred in the public interest.

Economies of scale in r. and d.

Some of the economies reviewed in the last two chapters have special application to r. and d.:

- research teams are only divisible down to a minimum effective scale;
- r. and d. is a type of set-up cost for new processes and products; and
- large diversified organisations have advantages in applying unexpected results of research.
- Small firms can attain these economies only to a limited extent by co-operating with one another.

Minimum effective scale. The advantage of large organisations in r. and d. is almost a matter of arithmetic. The average annual cost of r. and d. per scientifically qualified worker in manufacturing (excluding the aircraft industry) is about £10,000. The smallest team likely to show results would be 5 workers, costing £50,000. If 2 per cent of sales-turnover were spent on r. and d., sales would have to be £2·5 million to carry this effort. Sales of £2·5 million would normally involve a total workforce of more than 1500 men and women. R. and d. is simply beyond the means of small firms acting on their own.

The same point has been made by C. Freeman in connection with electronic capital goods.[1] It is estimated that the minimum r. and d. effort to evolve a new machine-tool control would cost £300–600 thousand. A small scientific computer would take £1–2 million. Spread over three years, £100–200 thousand would need to be spent each year on the control, and £333–666 thousand on the computer. It is estimated that a range of electronic data processing computers together with the associated software (programmes) would take £8–16 million: over 4 years, £2–4 million per year. A communications satellite would cost £10–40 million to develop over 5 years: £2–8 million per year. Only the largest firms can cross such thresholds.

Set-up costs. R. and d. work has one thing in common with setting up a machine shop in preparation for production: the task is the same whether the output is to be big or small. Large organisations have a decided advantage in that they can spread their costs of r. and d. over a large output.

Diversification. The large organisation has a further advantage in that it is well equipped to take advantage of the unexpected, and by the nature of research one cannot be sure in advance what the results will be. I.C.I., for example, have made discoveries in their dyestuffs division which were applicable in the plastics divi-

[1] C. Freeman, "Research and Development in Electronic Capital Goods", *National Institute Economic Review*, November 1965.

sion, discoveries in general chemicals that applied to insecticides, and so on.

It is not surprising that the Federation of British Industry found, in 1959, that 93 per cent of r. and d. expenditure was made by firms employing more than 2000 people.

Co-operative research. Small firms might assemble sufficient resources for r. and d. by joining together to form a co-operative research association. Such associations have been assisted by government subventions for fifty years; but they have not proved an adequate substitute for independent work. Small firms may increase in efficiency with the help of a research association. As all members have access to the same information at the same time, however, they can all advance together and are likely to quickly compete any gains away. A small firm cannot obtain any advantage *vis-à-vis* its rivals by co-operating with them, so enthusiasm for co-operation is apt to be tepid.

The concentration of r. and d.

It will be seen from Table 6 that 80–90 per cent of r. and d. in France, Germany, U.K. and U.S.A. is devoted to a narrow range

TABLE 6. Estimated Industrial Distribution of R. and D., 1962 (Percentages).

	U.K.	U.S.A.	Germany	France
Aircraft	35·4	36·3	} 19·5 (Aircraft, Vehicles, Machinery)	27·7
Vehicles	3·0	7·4		2·6
Machinery	7·3	8·2		6·4
Electrical machinery	21·7	21·6	} 33·8 (Electrical machinery, Instruments)	25·7
Instruments	2·3	3·9		—
Chemicals	11·6	12·6	32·9	16·8
Total	81·3	90·0	86·2	79·2

Source: C. Freeman and A. Young, *The Research and Development Effort*, O.E.C.D., Paris, 1965.

of industries making capital goods and chemicals, leaving only 10–20 per cent for basic materials and consumer goods. One reason for this concentration is to be found in the economies of scale discussed earlier. Capital goods and chemicals were produced by large firms before r. and d. became important, and the work of scientists and technologists has reinforced the advantages that size already conferred.

Two other reasons are extraneous to economics. Defence requirements have directed resources into these fields, and the growth of scientific knowledge has worked in the same direction. The basic scientific disciplines involved have been chemistry, electricity and mechanics, and these lead naturally into research on petrochemicals, plastics, fibres, transistors, atomic energy and jet propulsion. Many consumer goods and basic materials have been known for a long time during which knowledge about them has accumulated by trial and error.

Three further explanations of the concentration deserve consideration. Heavy r. and d. expenditures have been associated with

- oligopoly,
- growth, and
- the embodiment of technical advance in capital goods.

Oligopoly. It will be seen from Table 7 that capital goods and chemicals contain many fields in which there are only small numbers of competitors. Competition between a few may be in price, especially when there are marked changes in demand or costs, or when there is the threat of new entrants; but price reductions begun by one competitor may be quickly followed by another and get out of hand in the hurly-burly of a price-war. Hence price competition is often avoided by oligopolists. Instead they attempt to get ahead of one another by other means, among these by competing in innovation. If a firm is cleverer than its rivals it will gain at their expense, and so oligopolists are often willing to devote resources to r. and d.

In addition to willingness oligopolists may have the means to finance r. and d. in the form of high profits. R. and d. is akin to

TABLE 7. Concentration in Capital Goods and Chemical Industries, 1958.

Industry	Net output produced by 3, 4, 5 or 6 largest enterprises (per cent)	Number of enterprises
Dyestuffs	86·9	4
Fertilisers and chemicals for pest control	62·2	4
Explosives and fireworks	93·6	5
Soap, detergents, candles and glycerine	69·0	3
Synthetic resins and plastic materials	54·1	3
Steel tubes	82·8	5
Electrical machinery	54·1	5
Telegraph and telephone apparatus	58·4	3
Motor-cycle, three-wheel vehicle and pedal cycle manufacturing	56·6	3
Locomotives and railway track equipment	90·1	6
Railway carriages and wagons and trams	70·3	4
Production of man-made fibres	88·9	3

Source: *Census of Production, 1958.*

investment in that it is aimed at increasing earning power over future years. Unlike normal investment, however, it cannot usually be financed by borrowing as the prospects are too uncertain and there are few tangible assets to pledge as security for creditors. The money for r. and d. has almost always to be found from internal sources.

Growth. Table 8 places r. and d. expenditures as a percentage of net output and the growth of output alongside one another. It is evident that growth and r. and d. go together. The relationship may be seen as a virtuous circle: research leads to new products and techniques which stimulates demand which leads to growth in output which stimulates research which leads to new products and so on.

TABLE 8. R. and D. and Growth in the United Kingdom.

	R. and d. as % of net output (1959)	Growth of real output, 1935–58 (1935 = 100)
Aircraft	35·1	974
Electronics	12·8	503
Instruments	6·0	472
Vehicles and shipbuilding	1·4	213
All manufacturing	3·1	200

Source: C. Freeman, "Research and Development: a Comparison between British and American Industry", *National Institute Economic Review*, May, 1962.

Embodiment of technical advance. The incorporation of technological advance in capital equipment is implicit in this virtuous circle. Progress is mainly achieved by improving producer goods and so the concentration of r. and d. on such goods is to be expected.

The fact that technical advance is incorporated in plant and machinery means that productive capacity may grow by replacing old machinery with new without any investment beyond depreciation provisions. Growth is often associated with the "vintage" of capital equipment: the younger its equipment the more productive is an industry. "Vintage" is improved by r. and d.

How much r. and d.?

The association of r. and d. with large-scale production of capital goods and chemicals only takes one a little way towards answering the main economic question about r. and d.: how much should be spent on such work? Evidently, very little in a non-industrial community; but how much in a country well endowed with capital goods and chemical industries?

Formidable difficulties lie in the way of an answer. First, r. and d. is a very recent procedure in industry. In most firms such work only dates from the Second World War. Almost everybody who has been formally employed on industrial research is alive today and most are still quite young. We therefore lack experience in research management and the criteria to be employed in determining the size of research programmes. Secondly, research is by its nature unique. It always involves doing something that has never been done before, and so one can never be sure in advance that the work will be worth while. Thirdly, from the communal viewpoint, the money measure we use for evaluating change, the comparison of receipts and costs, only works well for small changes with existing products. If r. and d. always resulted in savings in cost for existing products, and factors of production were always saved in the same proportions, we should have no problems in measuring the return on such work and in determining its appropriate size. These conditions, however, are nowhere nearly met by such results of research as penicillin or the jet engine.

A precise answer being impossible, one can make some ranging shots: as a minimum, r. and d. should be sufficient to enable firms to keep pace with international competitors; as a maximum, it should not be on such a scale that investment cannot keep pace to incorporate the results. R. and d. work should not be premature. Results discovered before they are needed may be forgotten later, and these results might be achieved at lower cost after further accumulation of knowledge.

We must not do too much too soon, nor too little too late. To get beyond such generalities we can only rely on judgement. Some evidence on which judgement may be based is provided by international comparisons.

In Table 9, the r. and d. expenditures of U.K., U.S.A., Germany and France are compared. These expenditures are converted into £ sterling at official rates of exchange which give a false impression, especially in the case of U.S.A. $2.80 did not buy as much research effort in U.S.A. as £1 in U.K. because American salaries were higher and salaries represent about one-half of all r. and d. expenditures. If the U.S. figures are reduced by one-half, an extreme allowance, the U.S. lead in absolute expenditure remains formidable. And it is the work actually undertaken which matters, not its proportion to the population or to the Gross National

TABLE 9. Estimated Gross Expenditure on R. and D., 1962.

	£m. at official rates of exchange	£/head at official rates of exchange
U.K.	634	12
U.S.A.	6261	33
France	396	8
Germany	395	7

Source: C. Freeman and A. Young, *op. cit.*

Product. The U.S. expenditure represented 3·5 per cent of G.N.P. at factor cost, U.K. 2·6 per cent, France 1·8 per cent and Germany 1·5 per cent.

The size of r. and d. expenditure of U.S.A. is reflected in the "technological balance of payments" of U.K. In 1964, £24·4 million was identified as being paid to American firms as technological royalties, whereas only £6 million were identified as royalty receipts from U.S.A. On the other hand, the British technological balance with the world as a whole showed an excess of receipts over payments estimated at £3 million. Firms in the European Economic Community paid more in royalties to British firms than was paid in the opposite direction. The balance of receipts and expenditures is important as firms in Britain need to be of comparable technological strength with those abroad if full advantage is to be taken of patent agreements.

One further statistic may be mulled over. It is estimated that in 1966 scientists equal in number to 23 per cent of those qualifying three years earlier left U.K. with the intention of remaining abroad for a year or more. Engineers and technologists equal to 42 per cent of those qualifying three years earlier left U.K. with similar intentions. The British r. and d. effort was not held back for lack of suitably trained research workers.

When r. and d. in U.K. is compared with that of other countries, the outcome is no cause for complacency but it is not unfavourable. It also has to be remembered that r. and d. is not an unqualified good. The resources absorbed are valuable elsewhere, especially in education and current production. Employed in r. and d. resources are bound to be "wasted": many experiments prove abortive and many projects fail. In new technological fields there is often advantage in being second. There is no justification for chauvinism. If resources are to be devoted to the tasks in which they have a comparative advantage, it must often turn out that they will be devoted to conventional exports which serve to pay for the products of foreign r. and d.

Summary

● Large organisations have advantages in r. and d. because they can employ research teams which are big enough to be effective and can spread the costs over large outputs. Diversified firms can often find uses for the unexpected results of research.

● Co-operation does not allow small firms to put themselves on even terms with large ones, because the benefits of co-operative research are likely to be nullified by competition.

● Economies of scale, defence needs and scientific knowledge lead to concentration of r. and d. in capital goods and chemical industries. The working of oligopolistic competition and growth processes also make for such concentration.

● Criteria for determining the efficient size of r. and d. expenditure are difficult to lay down because of the uniqueness of each piece of work.

● R. and d. expenditures per head and as a proportion of G.N.P. in U.K. do not compare unfavourably with those of foreign countries; but in absolute terms U.S.A. has a long lead.

● R. and d. absorbs resources with alternative uses. The successes have to carry the costs of many failures. Results may be bought by conventional exports as well as by direct effort.

Reading

C. Freeman, "Research and Development: a Comparison between British and American Industry", *National Institute Economic Review*, May 1962.

APPENDIX: THE ECONOMICS OF PATENTS

Patents seem such an obviously desirable institution it is scarcely surprising that their merits have been debated by economists for more than a century. In Fig. 9 the stages in taking out a patent are set out in tabular form. The desirability of issuing patents has been questioned on the basis of monopoly theory. The monopoly argument is set out first and is followed by a brief review of the counter-arguments.

Patentee	Patent Office
Application and provisional specification lodged with Patent Office. Cost £1.	Formal mention in official journal.
Full list of claims, complete specification, must be filed within 12 months. Cost £10. Patent runs from this date.	
	Complete specification examined to determine: (a) whether it relates to manufacture or new method or process of testing applicable to manufacture; (b) whether it is new. If specification does not satisfy it is returned with stated objections.
Specification may be amended, e.g. claims restricted, or objections contested. Applications must be cleared within 2 years 9 months of filing complete specification.	When specification accepted, serial number issued. Final specification published, 3 months wait for objections.
Cost of sealing £3. Cases may now be brought for infringement of patent. After fourth year renewal fees must be paid, rising from £6 in 5th year to £30 in 16th year.	If no successful objection, application is sealed and patent granted.

FIG. 9. Stages in taking out a patent.

The monopoly argument against patents

A patent grants a statutory monopoly for a limited period. It is sometimes suggested that monopoly power may be extended in duration by a patentee taking out so many improvement patents that potential suppliers can never command sufficient of the technology to begin production. It is also alleged that monopoly power may be extended by implicit collusion between firms cross-licensing each other's patents. Monopoly power may even be built on a patent which could be successfully overturned, if a patentee can outspend would-be contestants in court. A patent may be a "licence to sue".

Patent monopolies are granted in order that patentees may enjoy higher profits than they would in free competition. In other words, they are intended to earn monopoly profits. This they can only do by restricting output below the competitive level. When inventions would be used whether or not patents were granted, then with patents output of patented goods will be lower and their prices higher than would be the case without patents.[1]

The possible misallocation of resources between patented and unpatented fields seems especially undesirable because, in the absence of patent legislation, the knowledge incorporated in an invention would be a free good. No-one is deprived of the employment of knowledge as a result of its use by others. Why then have patents?

Economic advantages of patents

Defenders of the patent system argue that it

- provides an incentive to inventors and so increases the amount of invention,
- permits disclosure of inventions,

[1] A popular argument against patents is that output may be restricted to zero: patents may be suppressed. This sometimes seems to be an everlasting argument about an everlasting match. It is completely out of date in countries, such as Britain, where the patent law provides for the compulsory licensing of patents that are not being commercially worked.

- reduces risks and so encourages the application of inventions, and
- is part of the process of competition in innovation.

The amount of invention. The obvious defence of patents is that they reward inventors, but it is not a strong defence. Some 70 per cent of patent applications in U.K. are made by companies. In the electrical and chemical fields company applications are an even higher percentage. Inventors are mostly paid salaries for their work. Invention is now an industrial activity.

Disclosure. The invention industry is likely to be most productive when there is quick disclosure of new discoveries, and the patent system provides for this. If an inventor has an idea in a thousand and it is published, then a thousand other inventors may seek the next elusive idea for an improvement. They are likely to hit upon something more quickly than the original inventor continuing on his own.

Protection of property rights in an invention upon its disclosure is necessary for the independent inventor if he is to be able to sell his invention. If inventors and their employers were obliged to work inventions themselves in secrecy, inventions might be used less and secrets might die with the inventor.

Application of inventions. The main justification for patents is to be found not at the stage of invention but at the later one of application. The absorption of resources in development work was discussed earlier. After an invention is fully developed large investment may be needed in production plant. It may not be profitable to use a new invention unless, by having a patent monopoly, the risk is reduced.

"*Test-tube competition.*" The introduction of new inventions is itself a competitive process, a "process of industrial mutation—if I may use that biological term—that incessantly revolutionises the economic structure *from within*, incessantly destroying the old one, incessantly creating a new one".[1] The monopoly argument with which we began is an excessively static one, concerned with the allocation of existing resources when the subject under discussion is the creation of new resources. The implicit picture is of numbers of firms sitting comfortably on their own patented islands, a picture that bears no relationship to the vulnerability of firms in new technological fields. Patents have provided modest comfort to firms engaged in atomic energy and electronic computers.

The danger may be that instead of stifling competition, patents may stimulate it too far. There is an opportunity cost to invention as to other activities, and we can have too much invention as well as too little. The patent system has the merit, however, of paying by results. There is a certain ingenuity in rewarding invention in this way.

Reading

Aubrey Silberston, "The Patent System", *Lloyds Bank Review*, April, 1967.

[1] J. A. Schumpeter, *Capitalism, Socialism and Democracy*, London, 1943, p. 83.

Chapter 4

AUTOMATION

SUPPOSE, as seems roughly true, that it takes £3 extra capital to increase output by £1 per year. The capital : output ratio is 3:1. Then one would expect that as capital per head increases over time by 30 per cent, output per head would increase by 10 per cent. In fact it is found to increase by about 100 per cent. There is a large increase in output, a "residual", that cannot be explained by increased capital.

This residual, or area of ignorance, is a splendid prize for special pleaders. Educationists argue that the unexplained increase in productivity is attributable to the improved quality of a better-educated labour force. Engineers may explain the residual by economies of scale, executives by better organisation and management, scientists by the accumulation of knowledge through research, and technologists by the embodiment of this knowledge in new plant and equipment.

There is probably something in each of these explanations. The economics of education is outside our province. Economies of scale, organisational economies and research and development have already been examined. This chapter is devoted to technological innovation.

It is difficult to be sober-minded about technology as men race to be first to land on the moon, and there has been much intoxicated verbosity. When the overblown claims are deflated, however, they remain of formidable proportions. The accelerating pace of innovation is illustrated in Fig. 10.

Innovation does not only follow invention and discovery more quickly than in the past: it is often bigger. Suppose change by factors of 10 is taken as the order of magnitude of technological

Innovation	Year of discovery	Year of application
Electric motor	1821	1886
Vacuum tube	1882	1915
Radio broadcasting	1887	1922
X-ray tubes	1895	1913
Nuclear reactor	1932	1942
Radar	1935	1940
Atomic bomb	1938	1945
Transistor	1948	1951
Solar battery	1953	1955
Stereospecific rubbers and plastics	1955	1958

FIG. 10. The increasing pace of innovation (from W. O. Baker, "The Dynamism of Science and Technology", in Eli Ginzberg, ed., *Technology and Social Change*).

advance. For example, if travel on foot is 4 miles per hour, by motor car 40 miles per hour and by jet-plane 400 miles per hour, then the motor car represents advance of one order of magnitude over walking and the jet-plane 2 orders of magnitude. On this scale the improvement in the speed of an electronic computer over hand calculation is an advance of at least 7 orders of magnitude: a 10-millionfold increase in speed over hand calculation.

Computers are one element in recent technological advances which have been collectively labelled "automation". These are the innovations on which this chapter concentrates. It explains what automation is, why firms automate, and the difficulties they face in automating; concluding sections examine the distribution of gains and losses and effects upon employment.

What is automation?

Automation consists of doing things more automatically. There are three main strands to such development: the use of

- transfer machines,
- automatic controls, and
- electronic computers.

Transfer machines. Transfer machines automatically feed work to other machines and automatically remove it for further processing. A typical example is the transfer line for machining engine-blocks of motor cars. This so-called "Detroit automation" does the sensing and manipulative work that previously was performed by human operatives. It is a fine engineering achievement, but historically it merely represents a recent stage of mechanisation.

Automatic controls. Automatic controls are of two types, programmed controls and closed-loop controls. Programmed controls put machines through predetermined sequences of operations. For example, the dials are set on an automatic washing-machine and the machine then proceeds to heat the water, and to wash, rinse and spin-dry the laundry. In a similar way, a paper tape is fed into a computer-controlled machine tool and the machine tool proceeds to deal with the metal as ordered.

Closed-loop controls represent a further technical advance. In a traditional plant gauges indicate performance and workers adjust controls to maintain standards. There is a gap between gauges and controls which is filled by the operative. This gap may at times be filled by devices which automatically compare performance with standards and automatically adjust controls to eliminate discrepancies (Fig. 11).

Simple closed-loop controls, such as the governor on a steam engine or the thermostat on a stove, have been used for many years. Recently it has become possible to install closed-loop controls of much greater sophistication so that parts of chemical plants and oil refineries can be kept performing with little human intervention.

Electronic computers. Closed-loop controls have led to talk, at times, of automatic factories; but they are not so exciting as the final ingredient of automation, electronic computers. It is true that computers are no better than morons capable of adding and subtracting on two fingers, but they perform these two operations at such speed that they have completely transformed many technological possibilities. Computers are used for two main purposes, process control and automatic data processing.

An example of process control may be found at the Samuel Fox steelworks at Stocksbridge. A computer calculates the best position to cut steel strip after it has been rolled from billets. The final length of the strip cannot be known until the tail-end has emerged from the rollers, when, with several hundred yards of steel moving at about 30 miles per hour, calculation of suitable lengths has to be

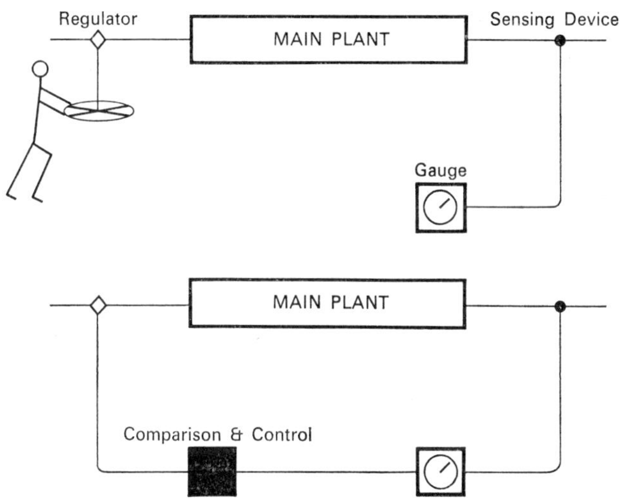

FIG. 11. Open and closed control loops.

done in seconds. Customer requirements are fed into the computer, which receives a signal of length of strip and works out least cost positions for three different stages of cutting. The computer measuring systems cost £60,000, and are said to save £40,000 per year.

Although process control by computer is impressive, the main gain from computers seems likely to be in the more mundane area of data processing. The typical place for automation is likely to be the office rather than the factory floor. The possibilities may once again be illustrated from the steel industry, this time by the Spencer Works near Newport. As orders are received from customers the details are fed into a computer, which calculates the tonnage of steel required at each stage according to normal yields. Orders are then grouped according to specification, delivery date, etc., to establish schedules for steel making. This information is fed to a second computer, which controls ingot and slabbing operations, and this in turn feeds into a third computer, which instructs regarding final rolling.

These developments seem so awesome that it may appear obvious that they be adopted as soon as demonstrated to be possible. Innovation, however, is never a question of technological possibility alone. It also has to be shown to be economic.

Why automate?

Automation makes possible improved products, as with the consistent quality of automatically mixed ice-cream, or, in a less trivial sphere, the more fully evaluated design of an aircraft. It also makes possible some products, such as atomic materials, which could not be made without automatic process controls. Information can be assembled and processed by computer that could not be dealt with in time by clerks using hand methods. The main contribution of automation, however, lies in reducing costs. utomation may

- reduce costs directly, and reduce them indirectly by
- improving the operating characteristics of plant, or by
- improving the working environment.

Direct cost saving. Automation is likely to reduce the number of operatives and maintenance men required per unit of output. Most of these workers usually need less skill and training. Equipment may cost less per unit of capacity, it may be used more fully and be maintained more easily. Less floor space may be needed with more productive plant. Set-up time may be curtailed, production periods shortened, and scrap losses reduced.

Operating characteristics. Machines are more predictable than people. Automation may, therefore, ease factory administration and production control. Output may be varied with little variation in the number of workers.

The working environment. The safest workplaces are probably the old-fashioned ones where traditional, slow methods are employed. Factory inspectors look most keenly at the up-to-date, high-speed plants. Machines mean danger, but more automatic machines mean less danger. Working conditions may be brighter, cleaner and more comfortable, and morale may be high when people have the latest equipment to work with.

The last three paragraphs have been spattered with "may be's", but if only a few of the potential advantages are realised they offer considerable economic inducement to automation. Unfortunately, difficulties may also be encountered.

Difficulties

Problems may be faced in

- designing and manufacturing automatic equipment,
- installing and learning to operate automatic plant,
- maintaining it in order, and
- managing it.

Equipment problems. Advanced equipment may be so productive that it saves capital as well as labour. At other times it is labour-saving alone, reducing current outlays at the cost of initial capital expenditure. In the latter case there may be problems of finance. These problems can be made worse by the long design times that are often needed for the new plant.

Automatic equipment is often highly specialised, designed to suit the specific requirements of one user. Making such equipment is "one-off" work and as such is not attractive to machine-tool manufacturers. They prefer to supply machine tools with wide markets, and so firms wishing to use highly automatic machinery often have to make their own.

Installation. Long design times have seldom, if ever, produced a plant which ran according to plan as soon as it was switched on. Bugs inevitably have to be removed. This process is made more difficult with labour-saving equipment as it has to be accomplished whilst workers are adapting to the new conditions.

Maintenance. Automatic plant has special labour requirements. The possibilities for saving unskilled labour are easily seen; but the saving of skilled labour may also be important. This often makes the most up-to-date equipment suitable for underdeveloped countries. Skilled operatives may be replaced by a smaller number of highly skilled maintenance men.

Maintenance crews need greater knowledge and skill, and they need supervision of high calibre. Maintenance work is of special importance as the cost of downtime increases with the productivity of plant: more output is sacrificed whilst the plant is out of use.

Management. This is one point at which management problems bite. Other problems arise because of the reduced flexibility of automatic plant. Production schedules are to a considerable extent built into the plant lay-out. There may be less flexibility in the sources from which raw materials are drawn, and less flexibility in the choice of products to make.

Just as the number of skilled operatives may be reduced by building their abilities into the machinery, so the number of middle managers needed may be reduced by automatic data processing which feeds information rapidly to top management. Middle managers are needed partly because the man on the spot knows most about what is happening and may reach decisions quickly; but the middle manager's special knowledge is being eroded. Top management must be more sophisticated but it needs fewer assistants. The narrowing of the promotion pyramid may make training and recruitment for top management more difficult.

There are thus disadvantages to set against the advantages of automation. As there is no compulsion to install automatic plant one would expect that it will only be chosen if the gains more than offset the costs. Who gets these gains?

The winners and losers

It should be borne in mind that economic competition may be the sort in which everyone wins a prize, and, if it seldom works out that way, it is usually the case that there are many more winners than losers. With technological advance there are gains in income and losses of jobs. How are these distributed?

The main gainers are the wage-earners who make the new equipment or work with it when it is installed. These men and women have their productivity enhanced and so they are worth paying higher wages. In addition to being paid more, they gain when they buy the products of technically advanced processes as these are progressively cheapened relative to other products.

A subsidiary group of gainers are those in jobs which feel no direct impact from technological change. These people do not supply the advanced sector with intermediate goods, nor are their products in close competition with those of the advanced sector in final markets. This group enjoy unchanged money incomes and lower prices for some of their purchases.

The third group, who are forced to change their jobs because they are displaced by machinery, join the second group for other innovations. When they are displaced, however, they are forced to move to jobs that they like less than the ones they have lost.

Automation and employment

In discussing changes of incomes we have talked of people losing their jobs but not of their losing employment. We assumed that other jobs are available. On the long view this must be true. Wages are paid because labour is in short supply relative to the demand. In communities that do not lack capital resources complementary to labour, there are always many jobs that might be filled in addition to those that are currently being performed. Looking back over history there has not, since the industrial revolution, been any problem of secular unemployment. The population of working age has grown steadily and so has the employed population.

Technological progress means increased output per unit of input, which leads to reduced prices and/or increased incomes. In any case purchasing power increases. Increased purchasing power leads to increased demand for output and so to new employment opportunities. Increased demand may be so great for the output of the advancing sector that people do not need to change their occupations. For example, the displacement of clerks by computers has led to no net reduction in the size of office staffs. In any case there will be increased demand to meet somewhere.

The employment problems posed by automation, therefore, are not of the cataclysmic sort that some latter-day Jeremiahs have prophesied. Man is in no danger of becoming as obsolete as the horse. The employment problems posed by automation are real, but they are transitional. They consist of the difficulties which may be faced when employment opportunities are changing more rapidly than the turnover of workpeople by retirement, juvenile recruitment and return to employment of married women. When large numbers of people with highly specialised skills, employed in narrowly localised activities, are made redundant, then the transitional problems are grave. Automation, however, is not a localised phenomenon.

At first it was thought that automation would mainly be a feature of industries using flow techniques: indeed that it might be confined to industries processing fluids. The idea was that with solid assemblies it might not be too difficult to fit two components together automatically, but to attach four components to those two would be more complicated, eight to those four even more complicated, and so on.

Many of the main examples of automation are to be found in industries using flow techniques: in oil-refining, chemicals, telecommunications, iron and steel, cement, paper, sheet glass, and food processing. But automation has also found its way into industries where it was claimed costs would be too high, management too dull or physical obstacles too great. There are examples of automation to be found in construction, mining, shipbuilding, distribution and transport. Automatic data processing may be applied anywhere.

Summary

- Increased output cannot be explained solely in terms of increased labour and capital. One important source of increase in productivity is technological innovation.
- Automation consists of doing things more automatically. There are three main methods: transfer machines, automatic controls and electronic computers.
- Automation may reduce the costs of materials, machinery or labour per unit of output, or it may reduce costs indirectly by improving operating characteristics of plant and the working environment.
- Difficulties are encountered in producing, installing, maintaining and managing automatic equipment.
- Technological advance means increased real incomes. These mainly accrue to those making or working with new equipment, but they are also diffused in reduced relative prices.
- There are always many more jobs that might be performed in addition to those currently being undertaken. Automation increases income and so the demand for output. It may give rise to frictional unemployment but not to long-term unemployment.

Reading

J. R. Bright, *Automation and Management*, Boston, 1958.

A. A. Alchian and W. R. Allen, *University Economics*, Belmont, California, 1964.

Chapter 5

MERGERS

THERE are as many synonyms for merger as there are for illicit love: absorption, acquisition, amalgamation, combination, fusion, take-over, to mention a few. To some extent this represents the needs of diplomacy. Directors of one company are apt to talk of "acquisition" amongst themselves whilst talking of "merger" to the directors of the company they aspire to control. It is possible to distinguish take-overs (or acquisitions) where company A offers cash or its own shares for shares in company B, has its offer accepted and company B disappears, from mergers (or amalgamations) where a new company C is formed to absorb companies A and B, shareholders in A and B accepting shares in C which survives whilst A and B disappear. From an economic point of view, however, these different routes to concentration of control are of little significance, and we shall use the various synonyms indifferently.

Economists have their own distinctions between forms of combination. These are first explained. The reasons for the large numbers of mergers in post-war years are then examined. Brewing is taken as an example of an industry where amalgamations have been especially popular. Brewing is also used as an example of the linking of successive stages of production, brewing and retailing. The chapter concludes with a discussion of the public interest in mergers.

Forms of combination

Mergers may be

- horizontal,
- chain,

- vertical,
- lateral, or
- conglomerate.

Horizontal mergers. These are formed between firms at the same stage of production, turning out the same product and selling in the same market. For example, the combination of Standard-Triumph–Leyland Motors with Rover Motors was horizontal: both firms assembled 2000 c.c. motor cars.

Horizontal merger is the form which gives rise most directly to monopoly problems. It has been feared by some that firms may join in horizontal combinations to continue restrictive practices without having to justify them before the Restrictive Practices Court.

Chains. Chains are formed by firms at the same stage of production, turning out the same product, but selling in separate local markets. The main examples are in retailing: the chains of grocers, shoe shops, chemists, variety stores and supermarkets, although many of these have been formed by growth rather than merger.

Chains take advantage of the fact that the same activities are repeated in different locations, and these may be planned more intensively from the centre than in any link of the chain. No single store of John Lewis, for instance, could afford the merchandising management it shares with the others. Some operations, such as buying, may also be centralised.

Vertical mergers. These differ from chains and horizontal mergers in that firms reach forward or backward or both to combine with others engaged in successive stages of production. The acquisitions of Fisher and Ludlow and Pressed Steel, both engaged in pressing car bodies, by British Motor Holdings are examples.

Vertical amalgamations are created to forge closer administrative links than can be provided by arm's-length dealing by purchase and sale of intermediate products. Backward integration often occurs in prosperous times when production is stretched and firms wish to ensure supplies of intermediate goods in order to maintain their own production. Forward integration may be undertaken to pre-empt access to markets when sales are difficult.

Lateral mergers. These are formed between companies engaged in producing related but not competitive goods. The take-over of Standard-Triumph Motors, making cars and light commercial vehicles, by Leyland Motors, at that stage engaged mainly on heavy commercial vehicles, is an example.

Lateral mergers arise because managements and staff possess knowledge and skills that are less specialised than the companies they serve. The same techniques of production may be applied in different fields, or distribution channels and sales forces may be used for related products.

Conglomerate mergers. Conglomerates are formed by combining firms making products that are not related in any way: for example, the merger of a book publisher with a manufacturer of oven glassware. These mergers are formed for diversification. They may be successful when undertaken in building up a financial holding company; but they give rise to many problems if management is intended to extend beyond finance.

The post-war years have witnessed every form of merger. The Board of Trade analysed the mergers undertaken, 1954–61, by quoted companies which numbered 2900 in 1954, a number which fell to 2600 in 1961 mainly because of combinations within the group. A smaller sample was analysed for the period 1962–3. This began with 2200 quoted companies and ended with 2000. Between 1954 and 1963 these companies acquired 5000 other companies, more than 600 acquisitions being public companies. Annual expenditure in shares or cash on acquisitions by public companies averaged £116 million in 1954 to 1958, £338 million in 1958 to 1961, and £345 million in 1962 to 1963. In 1962–3, about one out of every five or six quoted companies made at least one acquisition in a year: among the largest companies, with net assets exceeding

£25 million, about one in three companies made acquisitions in each year. Why has there been such a high rate of merger?

Reasons for mergers

Explanation must be sought in

- the "2 + 2 = 5" factor, or in what is really an aspect of this,
- the superiority sometimes of administration over market direction of resources.

"2 + 2 = 5". In order for a merger to be undertaken the participants must believe that the whole to be created will be greater than the sum of its parts. If two companies are to be combined, the shareholders in each must believe that proportionate shares in the combine will be worth more than their existing holdings. If one company is to take over another, it must value the acquisition more highly than the current owners, otherwise there would be a willing buyer but no willing seller.

The enhanced value may come from the creation of monopoly. Members of a combine do not need to compete with one another, and if they together control most of the market, then they may earn higher profits than they could separately. Attempts to monopolise lay behind some of the earliest mergers, in cement and wallpaper manufacture, in the 1890's. This element may still be found. For example, the Monopolies Commission objected to amalgamation between the Ross Group and Associated Fisheries because it was thought likely to limit competition.

Other sources of enhanced value may be found in earlier chapters. Mergers may be undertaken to achieve economies of scale, advantages of large organisations, scope for research and development, and opportunity for technological innovation.

Administration vs. the market. From one point of view, merger represents the replacement of market transactions by administrative arrangements. Marketing is costly. It involves product development, packaging, advertising, selling and physical distribution on the one side, and specification, purchase and chasing on the other. Closer and less costly control may sometimes be obtained by combining seller with purchaser. Administrative integration may replace market integration. This is especially the case with vertical mergers.

In the drink industry, with net assets of £894 million in 1960, net expenditure on acquiring subsidiaries, 1954–63, amounted to £247 million, i.e. 28 per cent of net assets. This industry led the rest in mergers. It is, therefore, the obvious one to choose in order to take a closer look at the considerations playing a part in mergers. The industry is also of interest in that brewing is one of the few where manufacture has been vertically integrated with retailing.

Brewing—an industry of mergers

The sums involved in acquiring subsidiaries reached such heights because of a number of very large take-overs, e.g. the payment of £20 million, wholly in shares, by Whitbreads for Flowers Brewery, and the payment of £19 million, 61 per cent in shares, by Courage, Barclay, Simonds for Bristol Brewery Georges. In addition there have been some spectacular mergers. For instance, Joshua Tetley merged with Walker Cain to form Tetley Walker (net assets £33 million) which merged with Ind Coope and Ansells to form Allied with £137 million assets.

In the very large mergers and take-overs it is difficult to disentangle the economics of the arrangements from personal reactions to the incursion of Mr. Eddie Taylor, the Canadian brewer, into a rather inbred "family" industry. The economic considerations may be more clearly seen in the less grandiose transactions that have been taking place continuously since 1945 as small local brewers have been absorbed by larger companies.

What may large brewing companies gain from acquiring smaller ones? From the point of view of a large company making an offer a take-over may

- provide a direction for competitive growth,
- enable transport costs to be reduced,
- lead to economies of scale, or
- provide opportunities for property development.

Competitive growth. Total consumption of beer fell from 38 million bulk barrels in 1914 to 25 million barrels of weaker beer in 1958. Since then consumption has risen to about 30 million barrels per year. For most of this century it has only been possible for an individual brewery to grow at the expense of its rivals. The total market has not been growing. It is not easy for an efficient brewery to compete a less efficient rival out of existence, however, partly because the size of the excise duty swamps attainable price reductions, and partly because more than two-thirds of sales of beer are made through public houses owned by brewers. An efficient firm therefore has to buy a larger market by taking over competitors and their tied houses.

Transport costs. Greater efficiency may be attained by larger brewers reducing transport costs. Transport, delivery and selling costs, together with the brewer's profit, make up about 18 per cent of the selling price of a pint of beer. Excise duty takes about 50 per cent, materials 7 per cent, and production costs 6 per cent (leaving a retail margin of 20 per cent). Moving reinforced water to and fro is expensive.

The small breweries built up their chains of tied houses in the days of the horse-dray. Larger areas may be covered by motor truck. Furthermore, deliveries do not need to be so frequent for bottled beer, with its long shelf-life, as for beer in barrel. Transport costs, therefore, only begin to offset economies of scale in brewing at a greater distance from the brewery than was true in the past. In addition to building up a larger marketing area by take-over, a brewing company may construct a cheaper transport network by filling in gaps between its existing retail houses.

Scale. Economies of scale at the brewing stage are not of overwhelming importance. The technological minimum size of an efficient brewery may be as small as 50–60 thousand barrels per year. Where there is excess brewing capacity, however, a single brewery may provide for a market formerly supplied by two.

Property development. Breweries were often sited in the middle of towns because of the need to minimise the cost of delivering the product. As time has passed the site value of the brewery has often risen. The same has happened with public houses occupying sites in high streets. Mergers which free a brewery site for alternative use or allow sales to be concentrated in fewer tied houses may offer large profits from property development. The most spectacular example was the Watney Mann merger that freed the Stag Brewery site at Victoria, London, for office development.

What is the attraction of merger to the smaller company? The fact that a large brewing company gains from a take-over would be sufficient to explain its taking place. The large company could offer a price greater than the present value of the smaller one as an independent concern. There are a number of additional incentives that a small company may have for accepting a take-over bid. A small brewing company frequently has difficulty in finding finance

- for developments in retailing, and
- to pay death duties.

Retailing. The finance needed for the brewing trade has risen markedly in post-war years. Licensed premises needed considerable sums spending on them in order to make them attractive for feminine as well as masculine custom and to develop catering facilities. There has also been the increased sale of beer in bottles, cans and kegs, which has involved large outlays for packaging plant and the replacement of coopers by capital investment in kegs. Sales of bottled and canned beer rose to two-fifths of total sales, and has since steadied at about one-third. One-twelfth of total sales are of keg beer.

Death duties. In addition to finance needed to operate there has been the need to cope with death duties. Most small breweries are private companies controlled by single families. If death of a principal shareholder occurred, the readiest means of paying duty would be to sell out to some other concern. The duty could be reduced in size by selling out before death and becoming the owner of land or shares with stock exchange valuations.

Integration of brewing and retailing

The small brewing companies have been fortunate in possessing readily saleable assets in the form of public houses and hotels. These usually make up about 80 per cent of the fixed assets, only 20 per cent being tied up in the brewery. There are 74,000 premises with on-licences in England and Wales, and brewing companies own 85 per cent of them. There are 26,000 off-licences, of which brewing companies own about 40 per cent. (In addition there are 21,000 registered clubs independent of the brewers.) The ownership of licensed premises, in 1967, by the biggest brewers is shown in Table 10.

Links between brewing and retailing are of such long standing that their exceptional nature may easily be overlooked. There are few other examples of integration forward from manufacturing to

TABLE 10. The Big Brewers.

	On- and off-licences
Bass, Charrington	11,000
Allied	10,300
Watney	8300
Whitbread	7400
Courage	5100
Scottish	1950

Source: The Times, 21.7.67.

retailing. Petrol refining and retailing is one of the few. Vertical integration in brewing has been undertaken because brewers

- supply a complete range of products,
- need close contacts with outlets and control over storage,
- can reduce transport costs by imposing delivery times,
- have had the finance available to acquire retail premises, and
- have faced restrictive licensing of retail outlets.

Range of products. One of the distinctive features of brewing is that the brewer supplies the main range of products sold by retail outlets. With one exception, brewers provide the whole range of beers required by the consumer: mild and bitter on draught, and pale ale, brown ale and stout in bottle. The exception, Guinness, is instructive as until very recently Guinness had no tied houses and brewed only stout. In most industries manufacturers make only a small part of the stock carried by their retailers, and so manufacturers would have to sell other people's wares as well as their own if they went into retailing.

Contact and control. Guinness also throws light on the need for close contact between brewer and licensee and for control of the licensee's stocks. Guinness is a high gravity beer, heavily hopped, which keeps longer than most other beers. Storage life is being increased by the introduction of kegs; but the main draught beers are not usually stored for more than two weeks, and so there is need for arrangements for speedy delivery from brewery to public house. When delivered the beer is still fermenting in the cask so there is need for skilled supervision of storage. Again, beer sales are markedly seasonal, sales in July and August being nearly double those of January and February, and demand changes rapidly with the temperature. Brewers need to know quickly of changes in demand. (Guinness, again the exception, is less seasonal in its sales.)

Transport. The need for speedy delivery emphasises the importance of transport; but public houses are not conveniently organised to take deliveries. The publican would much prefer to receive delivery outside opening hours. If delivery were confined to these times costs would be high, and so brewers gain by being able to persuade their tenants to take deliveries at times which will economise on transport. Transport is not only a matter of moving barrels and kegs. Bottles are carried out full and returned empty. Brewers re-use bottles 30 to 40 times, an economy which is achieved because most sales in bottle are made on licensed premises where empties are easy to retrieve.

Finance. Mention of bottles, which may represent a £750,000 investment to a large brewer, reminds one of the financial resources of brewers. Samuel Johnson overstated things when he claimed at the sale of Thrale's brewery: "We are not here to sell a parcel of boilers and vats, but the potentiality of growing rich beyond the dreams of avarice." Brewers have, however, enjoyed steady profits. They have been able to borrow money easily because the reliable profits guaranteed interest payments. In addition investment in licensed houses provided security for loans. Breweries have, therefore, always had the means to buy licensed houses when opportunity has offered.

Licensing. The licensing laws provided an incentive to such acquisitions because they allowed a brewer to pre-empt a local market, and prevented new entrants from building up trade by adding to the number of outlets. About 70 per cent of beer sales are made through tied houses.

Too big business?

Governments have not been bystanders as mergers have become more and more frequent. Nationalisation of an industry is, of course, merger by statute. Firms within the cotton textile, shipbuilding and aircraft industries have been encouraged to amalgamate by subsidies and financial inducements. The Industrial Reorganisation Corporation has been provided with £150 million of public funds to use to encourage mergers. On the other hand, the Monopolies Commission has been given power to investigate large mergers involving more than £5 million assets, and these mergers may be prevented from taking place. Governments have blown hot and cold in this way because the public interest is not wholly on the side of mergers. They may be a means for

- rationalising, or
- monopolising an industry.

Rationalisation. The rationalisation argument for merger may be applied to new science-based industries or to traditional declining industries. We have examined in earlier chapters the gains that may accrue in production, research and innovation to a large organisation. These are the considerations that have led to government encouragement of mergers in the aircraft and computer industries. The case for merger in declining industries rests on different grounds.

It used to be argued that the decline of an industry was no concern of the government. No-one had asked firms to join the industry, and if they made losses this was the price to be paid for the opportunity to make profits in more fortunate circumstances. If a firm went bankrupt, its plant and equipment might be bought cheaply and brought back into use at a lower level of costs. Existing equipment would be fully used and employment opportunities maintained. As equipment wore out it would not be replaced and the industry would gradually shrink to a size at which normal profits might once again be earned.

The trouble with this argument in favour of natural attrition is that it ignores the cumulative nature of decline. It also ignores the costs to workers made redundant. When capital equipment is durable, as was the case with the Lancashire loom, the contraction of an industry may be very slow. As it contracts it repels not only the managers and workers who are no longer needed, but also the enterprising recruits still required to replace some of the people retiring. Decline may cause further decline. There is thus a strong case for cutting declining industries quickly down to size and for providing compensation to the workers affected. Merger and concentration of production in fewer units may be the way to undertake such industrial surgery.

Monopoly. It is not always easy to distinguish a combination aimed at increasing efficiency from one aimed at restricting competition. Horizontal mergers may enable firms to control markets directly. Vertical mergers may give rise to monopoly indirectly. A vertical firm may discriminate in the sale of intermediate goods in favour of its own subsidiaries, or it may integrate forward into a market, such as public houses, where the number of outlets is limited. Vertical mergers are usually neutral in regard to monopoly, however, and the possibilities of monopoly by horizontal merger may easily be exaggerated.

In horizontal combinations the member firms often sell different ranges of products. If firms selling individually in low, medium or high quality markets combine, the effect on competition may be slight. The amalgamation of B.M.C. with Jaguar Motors, for example, had little effect on competition in the market for 1100 c.c. cars.

Horizontal mergers for monopoly are difficult to organise. It is in the interests of each firm to be the odd man out, enjoying high prices engineered by the combine without having to restrict its own output. The elimination of small competitors by underselling them is likely to be very expensive for a combine as it is likely to have to bear reduced prices on all its output. And new firms may enter a monopolised sector once monopoly profits are restored.

Summary

● Mergers may be horizontal, chain, vertical, lateral and conglomerate.

● They are undertaken when the whole can be made greater than the sum of its parts, sometimes because administrative integration may be more efficient than market integration.

● The brewing industry has been the scene of many mergers

because large companies when acquiring others find an avenue for growth, economise on transport, enjoy other economies of scale and develop properties; and small firms escape from the financial problems posed by developments in retailing and death duties.

● Brewers have traditionally linked production with wholesale and retail distribution by administration because they supply a complete range of products, need close contact with retail outlets, may reduce transport costs, have finance available, and face restrictive licensing of retail outlets.

● In assessing the public interest in mergers the benefits of rationalisation have to be weighed against possible reductions in competition.

Reading

W. E. Alberts and J. E. Segall, *The Corporate Merger*, Chicago, 1966.

P. L. Cooke and R. Cohen, *Effects of Mergers*, London, 1958.

J. Vaizey, *The Brewing Industry*, London, 1960.

Chapter 6

THE SURVIVAL OF SMALL FIRMS

THE discussion so far mostly helps to explain the predominance of large firms. They may employ more efficient techniques of production than small firms, and, if none of these exist, there are no techniques of small firms that bigger ones cannot employ many times over. There may be further advantages in large-scale organisation, in research and development, and in innovation. Consequently there have been widespread mergers. Large organisations may run into problems of co-ordination, control, communications and morale; but these problems may be overcome.

There is a danger of seeming to explain too much. 500,000 shops and 350,000 agricultural holdings are mainly of modest size, and, confining attention to manufacturing, 92 per cent of establishments have fewer than 100 employees and provide work for 26 per cent of all manufacturing employees. A company may own more than one establishment. The average is 1·3 establishments per firm; but multi-plant firms probably own more large establishments, so figures for size of establishment correspond fairly well with those for units of control.

The facts that most manufacturing establishments are small and provide work for a significant proportion of employees are not peculiarly British. In the United States, 91 per cent of all manufacturing establishments, providing work for 27 per cent of all manufacturing employees, have fewer than 100 employees; in West Germany the percentages are 89 and 27; in New Zealand, 97 and 62; in Argentine, 98 and 52; in Japan, 98 and 56.

This chapter discusses the characteristics of small-scale industry and then examines the strengths and weaknesses of small firms.

Characteristics of small-scale industry

Products. The products supplied on a small scale usually have one or more of the following features.

- The national market may be limited in size, as with leather-goods and lace. Luxury items are usually supplied by small firms, e.g. hi-fi equipment.
- This feature may be more marked. There may be no national market, but only a regional one: some cheeses and black puddings provide examples. Building, with a completely localised market, gives scope for many small firms.
- Products that are made in special lots or in short runs are often made by small firms. For example, foundries are often small.
- High-precision work is also often performed on a small scale. This may be because of the size of the market, but it also stems from the need for close supervision of such work. Firms making instruments, for instance, are often small.
- Simple products may often be mass produced by small firms. For example, a firm employing 60 people could enjoy all the economies of scale from mass producing table knives.
- When sections of industry have different rates of growth, slow-growing sectors may provide opportunities for small firms. The provision of bolt-on parts to raise the performance of motor car engines is an example.
- Finally, firms selling services are often small. The major cost in service trades is labour, and, as services are usually provided by individuals or small teams, the large firm has no advantage. Repair work is often undertaken by small firms.

Industries with very small establishments. Bearing these features in mind it is not surprising that industries containing very small firms should be concerned with bacon curing and sausages, bread and flour confectionery, canvas goods, fish curing, furs, gloves, hair and fibre goods, lace, leathergoods, mechanical engineering repairs, soft drinks, and timber.

Industries with small establishments. Moving into a slightly larger size-range, there are small establishments concerned with wholesale bottling, brick and fire-clay products, building materials, flock and rags, laundry, dry-cleaning, job-dyeing, carpet beating, leather tanning and dressing, made-up household textiles, milk products, non-metalliferous mining and quarrying, publishing, scrap metal processing, soft furnishing, and wooden container manufacturing.

Sources of strength

Small firms only need to be as efficient as larger rivals, they need not be more efficient. There is a temptation to think of *the* optimum size of firm in an industry, but the many forces bearing on firms make such a single best size unlikely. In place of the idea of an optimum a principle of equal eligibility may be maintained, that firms of varying sizes may be equally fitted for survival in competition with one another.

Small firms may draw strength from

- low transport costs,
- external economies,
- management,
- morale, and
- flexibility.

Transport costs. Small firms may gain because their products do not incur large transport costs. For example, wholesale bottling is listed above as an industry with small establishments. It is also an industry with a highly automated plant bottling Ind Coope beer; but the price of automation is that beer has to be transported long distances in bottle, and empty bottles have to be transported long distances back to the plant. Smaller bottling plants predominate because they can receive beer in bulk and bottle for their local areas.

External economies. There are further economies related to transport economies that arise from the mutual strength neighbouring firms may confer on one another. In localised industries firms may specialise in sections and stages of production, meeting their needs by buying from other firms undertaking complementary activities. Areas such as Sheffield or the Black Country resemble huge manufacturing enterprises with small firms corresponding to small departments in unitary organisations.

Management. Looking within small firms, there may be gains in management, morale and flexibility. Management, as will be seen later, may be a source of weakness, but it is often a source of strength. In a small firm it is easy for the manager to know all that is going on simply by looking: there is no need for elaborate production scheduling, cost controls, stock controls, current and capital budgeting in order that activities may be co-ordinated and waste avoided.

Avoidance of waste comes naturally as incentives are simple and direct. Ownership and management are usually identical or closely connected. The manager is looking after his own money and this is different from looking after other people's money. I remember suggesting to the manager of a small firm some doubt about whether firms attempt to maximise profits: he replied that he would as soon doubt the law of gravity.

Identity of ownership and control means family ownership and control and family succession in management. Any Lancastrian can quote "three generations, clogs to clogs", but nepotism has some advantages as a system of management recruitment. It is often less difficult to give early responsibility to a son, son-in-law or nephew than to an outsider, and this is a very effective means of management training. Furthermore, small-scale business is not just a means of making a living, it is also a way of life offering independence, with no-one to answer to but himself, to the boss. A small firm may therefore be attractive to a man with ability to manage something very much bigger.

Morale. The attraction may extend to the weekly wage-earner. A small firm imposes fewer formal restraints on workers. They are treated as individuals and can see what their work contributes to the total output. Some years ago I asked a trade unionist to show me the worst working conditions in the cutlery trade. The effect of his demonstration was somewhat reduced by the fact that the workshop was to be closed the following week; but it was certainly a dark, satanic place with women buffing spoons in a fog of black dust. The buffers wore paper shawls and aprons and were covered from top to toe in dust. Yet this workshop had a full complement of workers whilst larger firms went short. The women liked working with one another, kept their own times, and fitted shopping and other family demands into the day to suit their convenience.

Flexibility. Working hours are only one type of flexibility within a small firm. A small firm with a simple organisation and limited commitment to specialised equipment is much more manœuvrable than its larger competitors. Small firms therefore flourish where quick responses to opportunity have to be made. They have a special advantage in fashion trades. Small firms are also found in the trades where work changes from day to day as with building repairs and mechanical repairs.

Weaknesses

There are more than 2000 bankruptcies and 400 compulsory liquidations each year. An unknown number of firms fold up quietly, and many small firms hang on offering their owners a lower return on their capital and lower remuneration for their work than they would get if they invested and sought employment in a larger organisation. Small firms have weaknesses as well as strengths:

- vulnerability,
- weak management,
- lack of finance,
- exposure to personal taxation,
- inadequate research and development, and
- inability to advertise.

Vulnerability. It is easy for a small firm to fail. One set-back can be a disaster. I.C.I. could lose £2 million on a synthetic fibre made from coconuts and offset the loss against profits elsewhere, regarding such misfortune as part of the cost of being an innovating firm. In a small firm, failure of a product, loss of a market, or breakdown of plant may be the end.

This vulnerability is increased by the fact that in a small firm management is the performance of a few people rather than of an impersonal organisation. In a large firm the management does not get ill or die, but in a small firm it may. Moral hazards are also more serious for small firms. Nine out of ten bankruptcies are because of drink, gambling or women.

Management. There are other problems with small-scale management. It calls for all-rounders and abilities may be specialised. An individual may be strong on production or marketing or personnel or accounts, but to ask that he show flair in all aspects of a business is to ask a great deal. In many small firms managers are so tied up with immediate operations that they have no time for the long-term plans on which prosperity might be built.

Long-term considerations bring us once more to management succession and nepotism. Nepotists may give early opportunities to their kith and kin, but they are obviously limited by the number of their relatives. A small businessman needs a lot of sons, in the hope that one of them will turn out to have managerial ability, or a lot of daughters, in the hope that one of them will marry managerial ability. Whatever the size of his family, this process for finding a successor is far from fool-proof.

Finance. Financial problems are linked to the vulnerability and personal management of small firms. When so much depends upon who the manager is, outside finance is limited to whom the manager knows. Institutions which seek to aid small firms, such as the Industrial and Commercial Finance Corporation, are obliged to eschew the smallest loans because the cost of investigating such projects would be more than the loan could be worth to the borrower.

Limited sources of finance are often made more constricting by rudimentary accounting. If insufficient attention is paid to the cash flow, the difference between liquidity and solvency may be discovered in business failure. This is especially a problem when a small firm is growing fast. When sales expand fast a firm may have lots of money due to it but lack the wherewithal to pay its own bills.

Problems of liquidity also arise at times of general financial stringency. If banks are obliged to restrict credit, their smallest customers are likely to suffer most, not because they are inefficient, but because they are the most dependent on bank finance. The fattest rather than the fittest may survive.

Taxation. It is difficult to determine the extent to which taxation makes financial problems more difficult than they used to be. High taxes have been accompanied by high profits, and so ability has grown with the necessity to pay. The tax which has special impact on family businesses, death duty, may be avoided. The dependence of small firms on internal finance, however, means that they are likely to find taxes particularly burdensome.

Research and development. It was seen in Chapter 3 that there are considerable economies of scale in r. and d. The obverse of this is that small firms are at a disadvantage in science-based industries. Small firms may have bright ideas and base innovation upon them; but they cannot hope to compete in areas where step-by-step research is necessary or expensive development has to be undertaken.

Advertising. The threshold to be crossed may be as high in advertising as in r. and d. The Animal Trap Company of America demonstrated that if you build a better mousetrap the world does not beat a path to your door.[1] There have been cases where a new

[1] See J. B. Matthews, R. D. Buzzell, T. Levitt and R. E. Frank, *Marketing*, New York, 1964, pp. 3–6.

product has swept the market on the basis of word-of-mouth recommendation. The Wilkinson stainless steel safety-razor blade was a notable one. It was also exceptional.

Summary

● More than 90 per cent of the firms in manufacturing each employ fewer than 100 people, and whilst they each contribute little together they account for more than one-quarter of manufacturing employment.

● Small firms make products with limited national volume or regional markets. They make goods in short runs or special lots, and undertake high-precision work. They mass produce simple goods, cater for slowly growing segments of industry, and supply services.

● Small firms may enjoy low transport costs and external economies. Management is straightforward, incentives to high performance are direct, and family succession may confer early responsibility. Morale may be high. Response may be quick to new opportunities.

● On the other hand, failure is easy, management may be weak, finance is constricted, taxation may be onerous, and r. and d. and advertising may be out of reach.

Reading

E. Staley and R. Morse, *Modern Small Industry for Developing Countries*, New York, 1965.

PART TWO

Monopoly—The Pragmatic Approach

INTRODUCTION

MONOPOLY intruded into the consideration of efficiency and scale in Part One as a feature of patent legislation and as a possible reason for horizontal and vertical mergers. Just as monopoly could not be kept out of Part One, economies of scale, organisational economies, research and development and technological innovation cannot be kept out of Part Two, which is devoted to an examination of monopoly and its control.

Monopoly and competition should not be seen in black and white, with black for monopoly and white for competition. Firms have monopolistic and competitive features, and these are associated in both cases with desirable and undesirable characteristics. The picture is a study in greys. Monopoly is a matter of degree. This may be seen in the nature of monopoly and the measurement of monopoly power, which form the subject matter of Chapter 7. Chapter 8 is concerned with the merits of monopoly and resale price maintenance, and the identification of monopoly profits. Chapter 9 is devoted to the Monopolies Commission and the Restrictive Practices Court, two public bodies established to examine monopolies and monopolistic practices on their merits. Monopoly is a subject for pragmatism, not dogmatism.

Chapter 7

THE NATURE AND MEASUREMENT OF MONOPOLY POWER

BEYOND being a term of abuse, monopoly may refer to a type of market structure, to forms of behaviour or to resistance to change. These three meanings are examined in the first section. A second section is devoted to the measurement of monopoly power.

The nature of monopoly

A monopoly may consist of a single firm or a group of firms acting together. When a number of firms act together they may do so by explicit or implicit agreement. The firm or group may be distinguished as a monopoly because they

- form a type of market,
- behave in special ways, or
- constitute an impediment to the selection of the fittest.

Market structures. A firm or group may be regarded as a monopoly because they face product demand which is more than proportionately responsive to changes in the product's price, and completely unresponsive to changes in other prices. They do not expect other firms to alter prices because of any changes they make themselves, and they are completely protected from entry of new producers into the market.

This contrasts with a perfectly competitive market structure, consisting of a large number of firms making identical products, where individual firms face demand which would be very responsive to price changes. There would be a large change in the demand for one firm's product as a result of changes in its competitors' prices. Perfect competitors would have no more need than monopolists to conjecture about the response of rivals to price changes; but newcomers would be completely free to enter the market.

In monopolistic competition, where large numbers of firms make products differing only slightly from one another, individual firms would experience demand which was more responsive to own price changes than with monopoly and less than with perfect competition. Demand response to changes in rivals' prices would also be intermediate. Conjecture about price responses of large numbers of monopolistic competitors would be as pointless as in the first two markets. Entry would be easy but not completely free as with perfect competition.

The fourth main market structure is oligopoly, competition between a few firms, which is distinguished by the fact that an individual firm may face a demand highly responsive to price increases that rivals need not follow, but not very responsive to price reductions that rivals must match. Demand would be very responsive to price changes of rivals. Each firm would expect rivals to change their prices in response to its own price adjustments; and entry would be impeded.

These distinctions may be made more precise by measuring the responsiveness of demand to own price changes by the elasticity of demand (the ratio of the proportionate change in the quantity demanded to the proportionate change in price), and to other price changes by cross-elasticity of demand (the ratio of the proportionate change in the demand for one commodity to the proportionate change in the price of another). Expectations with regard to competitors' price changes as a result of one firm changing its prices may be measured by conjectural price flexibility (the ratio of the expected proportionate change in a rival's price to the proportionate change in one firm's price). Entry may be considered free, impeded or blocked. Using these measures, the distinctions between market structures are tabulated in Fig. 12.

It will be seen from Fig. 12 that monopoly is a matter of degree.

	Elasticity of demand	Cross-elasticity of demand	Conjectural price flexibility	Entry
Monopoly	greater than unity but small	very small	zero	blocked
Perfect competition	very large	very large	zero	free
Monopolistic competition	large	large	zero	impeded
Oligopoly	large for price increase and small for price reduction	large	unity or greater	impeded

FIG. 12. Defining characteristics of various market structures. Cross-elasticities are with reference to close competitors: low cross-elasticities define market boundaries.

Every commodity competes with every other for consumers' limited incomes, so cross-elasticities of demand can never be zero. Barriers to entry vary in height but are seldom insurmountable. Firms often supply several markets and their monopoly power may be different in each. For example, the electricity authorities have statutory monopolies for the public supply of electricity. There are only poor substitutes for electricity for lighting and hence the cross-elasticity of demand between electricity and other sources of artificial light is small. On the other hand, coal, gas and oil may be substituted for electricity for heating and power, and in these uses the cross-elasticity of demand between electricity and other fuels is large. The barrier to entry is not absolute despite the nationalisation statute in that firms may generate electricity for themselves.

Technical distinctions between market structures are the basis of predictions of outputs, prices and profits. It is argued that with monopoly output will be lower, prices higher and profits larger than would be the case with production in other types of market. These predictions sometimes prove false, and monopolists are accused of lethargy, inefficiency, high costs and consequently modest profits. When these accusations are made it is evident that monopoly refers to forms of behaviour, or to absence of competitive behaviour, rather than to a market structure.

Monopoly behaviour. When competition is intense firms have little choice but to strive to get ahead of one another. Otherwise they may go to the wall. A monopoly is less constrained. Instead of exploiting the position for high profits, the management may contentedly pursue a quiet life.

There are other possibilities. The aim may be to maximise sales subject to the maintenance of a satisfactory rate of profit. This might ensure the continued absence of competitors and provide justification for increasing managerial salaries. It might result in a monopoly producing an output little smaller than that with perfect competition and selling it at low price. Alternatively, management may aim at a minimum rate of growth or a high rate of innovation. Monopoly behaviour cannot be deduced from a market form. It has to be discovered by observation.

Social friction. Monopoly matters not only because of its impact on the behaviour of individual firms but also because of its influence on the general working of the economy. Competition may be viewed as a means for organising the millions of bits of specialised knowledge of production possibilities and market opportunities spread throughout the population so that resources are put to their most productive uses. We discover what to produce and how to produce by allowing everyone to interpret the restrictions represented by costs and the demands reflected in factor and product prices. Right interpretations lead to prosperity and wrong ones to losses. The whole system may be regarded as a means for selecting the fittest economic organisations for survival.

The working of this system is subject to a number of well-known limitations, one of which is provided by monopoly. A monopoly may receive high prices for its products relative to their costs. Consumers signal that they would prefer to have more resources devoted to making its output. The monopoly may continue its existing level of output in order to maximise profit. Resources have to be devoted to less-preferred uses elsewhere. The monopoly output is too small and output elsewhere too large.

Alternatively, the monopoly may waste resources and incur high costs. If it faced direct competitors it would be eliminated for such behaviour; but in its protected position it can survive. Monopoly may, therefore, be regarded as a factor increasing the friction in the working of the economic system.

Monopoly is thus a recognisable rather than a precisely defined market structure. It encompasses a range of behaviour, and provides a larger or smaller impediment to the market direction of resources. Firms may have more or less monopoly power. This suggests attempts to measure it.

The measurement of monopoly power

It has been proposed that monopoly power be measured

- price/cost ratios,
- cross-elasticity of demand,
- the ratio of the rate of profit to the rate of interest, and
- concentration ratios.

Price/cost ratios. In perfect competition price would equal marginal receipts and so, with profits being maximised where marginal receipts equal marginal costs, price would equal marginal costs. With monopoly price would be lower at larger outputs, so marginal receipts would be less than price and price would exceed marginal cost. Hence A. P. Lerner proposed that monopoly power be measured by the ratio of the difference between price and marginal cost to price.

$$\text{Monopoly power} = \frac{\text{price} - \text{marginal cost}}{\text{price}}$$

The Lerner Index would equal zero with perfect competition and be positive with monopoly. However, it is far from satisfactory. Its size depends partly upon the elasticity of demand, which is only indirectly related to monopoly power, and partly upon the level of costs, which may be high, and reduce the index, when monopoly power is large. The index fails to take account of the absolute size of market served. For example, the index might be the same for tuning forks and plate glass; but one would not wish to say that the market power of Ragg Tuning Forks equals that of Pilkingtons. The index provides no indication of the possibility of new competitors entering an industry. Finally, its calculation requires information which is not usually available.

Demand cross-elasticity. The cross-elasticity of demand was employed above as one of the defining characteristics of market structures. It is very low for a monopoly and very high for a firm in perfect competition. As monopoly power depends upon the absence of substitutable supplies, and as cross-elasticity falls with falling substitutability, use of cross-elasticity of demand as a measure of monopoly power is attractive. The weakness of this measure is that it fails to take account of the behaviour of small numbers of competitors. For example, the cross-elasticity of demand between Unilever and Proctor and Gamble detergents must be large; but it would be unreal to attribute small market power to these two companies.

Ratio of profit to rate of interest. The third measure is based on the idea that in competitive equilibrium economic profit would be zero, and accounting profit would equal the rate of interest. Using the ratio of economic profit to the rate of interest, we would once more have a measure which equals zero with perfect competition. Unfortunately, a monopoly might earn no economic profit because it suffered from inflated costs or chose to maximise sales. And economic profit may arise for other reasons in addition to monopoly. The identification of monopoly profit is discussed in the next chapter.

The first three methods of measurement were all suggested by economic theorists. They may seem excessively theoretical, but it must be borne in mind that the behaviour of costs, availability of substitutes and size of profits all need to be taken into account in monopoly investigations. The fourth measure was put forward by descriptive economists.

Concentration ratios. A concentration ratio is the percentage of employment, gross output or net output attributable to the three largest, four largest or eight largest firms in an industry. The number of firms determining the percentage usually depends upon the smallest number that official statisticians are prepared to classify together in view of their obligation to maintain the anonymity of firms supplying returns in censuses of production. In the U.K. the number is three. For example, in 1958, the three largest oil companies provided 88 per cent of the net output of mineral oil refineries, whilst the three largest firms making dresses and lingerie supplied only 3 per cent of net output. Concentration ratios may at times be given in inverse form by stating the cumulative total of firms arranged in decreasing order of size which together supply a particular percentage of net output or account for a particular percentage of employment.

Concentration ratios seem revealing statistics, but they are not free from problems. The statistics on which they are based are collected for standard industrial classifications, and these often do not correspond to the markets in which an economist is interested. For instance, men's and women's shoes are provided by one statistical industry but they are sold in separate markets. Again the statistics are usually national ones, and a low national concentration ratio may conceal regional monopoly power. Bricks, bread and beer are sold regionally.

The top three firms may remain the same over time or membership may change rapidly. In the latter case high concentration does not indicate great power. The size of the top three firms relative to one another may make a considerable difference. In one industry with a 75 per cent concentration ratio, the three firms may each supply 25 per cent of output; in another the largest firm may supply 65 per cent and the other two 5 per cent each. The total number of firms in an industry matters as well as their market shares because the possibility of collusion depends partly on the number of participants, and even with modest concentration ratios firms may agree to act together. Finally, the presence of foreign competition may radically change the significance of high national concentration.

Despite their limitations concentration ratios are of considerable practical importance. The statutory definition of a monopoly is a firm supplying more than one-third of the market. Concentration ratios are regularly compiled statistics which provide an indication of the possibility of monopoly conditions and of changing conditions over time.

The most thorough investigation of industrial concentration in Britain was that undertaken by Evely and Little in their analysis of statistics made available by the 1951 Census of Production.[1] They took account of the size of the top three firms relative to the rest by dividing trades into two groups: a large-size group where the three largest business units were sixteen or more times as big as the remainder, and a second group where the three largest were fifteen or less times as large. They took account of the number of firms in an industry by classifying trades into those with few business units (30 and under) and many units (31 and over). Finally, they distinguished between trades with high concentration ratios, 67 per cent and over, medium concentration, 34–66 per cent, and low concentration, 33 per cent and under.

Out of 219 trades analysed, only 20, accounting for 3·3 per cent of total employment, fell into the class with high concentration, few business units, and large relative size of the top three firms. A further 13 trades, accounting for another 4 per cent of total employment, were highly concentrated but had a large fringe of small firms, although the top three firms were relatively large. These 33 trades are the ones with high probability of monopoly. The

[1] R. Evely and I. M. D. Little, *Concentration in British Industry*, Cambridge, 1960.

first twenty were transmission chains, motor cycles, internal combustion engines, sugar and glucose, primary batteries, explosives and fireworks, wallpaper, notepaper, pads and envelopes, precious metals refining, abrasive wheels, small arms, photographic plates and films, razors (excluding electric), accumulators, scales and weighing machinery, seed crushing and oil refining, cotton thread, incandescent mantles, margarine, and matches.

At the other end of the scale, Evely and Little found 29 trades, accounting for 6·4 per cent of total employment, with medium concentration, many business units, and small-size ratio of the largest to the rest. Sixty trades, with 20·8 per cent of total employment, had low concentration, many units, and small relative size of the three largest firms. These 89 trades, with 27·2 per cent of total employment, were probably highly competitive. The full analysis is given in Table 11. The top ten and bottom ten trades for concentration in 1958 are listed in Table 12.

Evely and Little's work indicates that monopoly is not so widespread in manufacturing industry as talk of monopoly capitalism might suggest. When there is monopoly it may not be undesirable. It will be seen in the next chapter that monopolies have advantages as well as disadvantages.

Summary

● Monopoly may refer to a market structure which, with profit maximisation, is associated with restricted output, high prices and high profits. Structural analysis suggests investigation of conditions of entry, demand and costs.

● In intense competition participants have no choice but to attempt to get ahead of one another simply to stay in the game. Monopoly may refer to the wider range of behaviour possible as pressure from others diminishes.

● When everyone competes with everyone else the combined outcome is a social system which integrates the specialised knowledge spread throughout the community. Monopoly impedes the working of this system.

TABLE 11. Distribution of 219 Trades according to Degree of Concentration, Number and Size Ratio of Units.

Concentration	Large size-ratio of units (16 and over)				Small size-ratio of units (15 and under)				Total	
	Few units (30 and under)		Many units (31 and over)		Few units (30 and under)		Many units (31 and over)			
	No. of trades	% of total employment	No. of trades	% of total employment	No. of trades	% of total employment	No. of trades	% of total employment	No. of trades	% of total employment
High (67% and over)	20	3·3	13	4·0	17	3·4	—	—	50	10·7
Medium (34–66%)	—	—	25	17·5	15	2·0	29	6·4	69	25·9
Low (33% and under)	—	—	40	42·6	—	—	60	20·8	100	63·4
Total	20	3·3	78	64·1	32	5·4	89	27·2	219	100·0

Source: R. Evely and I. M. D. Little, *Concentration in British Industry*, Cambridge, 1960. Statistics are for 1951.

TABLE 12. Industrial Concentration, 1958: the Top Ten and Bottom Ten.

	Percentage of net output by 3 largest firms
Man-made fibres	89
Mineral oil refining	88
Locomotive and track equipment	60–82
Tobacco	81
Sugar	79
Explosives and fireworks	75
Dyestuffs	74
Margarine	71
Cement	70
Soap, detergents	69
Overalls, shirts, etc.	8
Furniture and upholstery	8
General printing and publishing	8
Household textiles	7
Miscellaneous metal goods	7
Wooden containers and baskets	7
Miscellaneous wood/cork products	6
Timber	4
Construction	4
Dresses, lingerie, etc.	3

Source: Census of Production, 1958.

● Price/cost ratios, cross-elasticity of demand and the ratio of profit to the rate of interest have been suggested as measures of monopoly power. These suggestions are followed up in a rough and ready manner by investigators who examine the behaviour of costs, availability of substitutes and level of profits.

● Concentration ratios provide a means of sifting industrial statistics as a first step in discovering the presence of monopoly.

Reading

F. A. Hayek, *Individualism and Economic Order*, London, 1949.

R. Evely and I. M. D. Little, *Concentration in British Industry*, Cambridge, 1960.

Chapter 8

THE MERITS OF MONOPOLY

Knowledge of the advantages and disadvantages of monopoly has a proverbial flavour. Just as proverbs come in off-setting pairs—"too many cooks spoil the broth", "many hands make light work"—so each disadvantage may be matched by a possible advantage. These are discussed in the first section. This is followed by consideration of resale price maintenance and a final section devoted to the identification of monopoly profit.

The desirability of monopoly

A monopoly may

● stagnate, making old-fashioned products by old-fashioned methods, or

●● it may be in the van of technical progress with monopoly profits providing the finance for research and development: the monopoly itself may be based on patents.

● A monopoly may suffer all the disadvantages of large organisations, or

●● it may enjoy economies of scale as is most obviously the case with natural monopolies such as gas and water supply.

● It may be associated with the misallocation of resources, output being too small and prices too high, or

●● it may improve the use of resources by making available more information on which to base decisions, and by removing the risk of capacity being duplicated.

● It may lead to firms accumulating excessive profits, but

●● the owners of monopolies may be worthy bodies, e.g. pension funds or the Church Commissioners.

● Monopoly may necessitate the introduction of political checks on operations to replace the market check of competition, or

●● it may itself be a checking device, the power of one monopolist countervailing that of another.

● Finally, from a narrowly nationalistic point of view, a monopoly may be particularly undesirable because it is a foreign one charging high prices to importers, or

●● it may improve the terms of trade by being a domestic monopoly selling abroad.

Technological progress and economies of scale have been sufficiently examined in earlier chapters. Monopoly profits are discussed at the end of this chapter. The allocation of resources, countervailing power and terms of trade are considered at once.

Resource allocation. The misdirection of labour and capital caused by monopolistic restrictions have been commonplaces of price theory for a long time. Recently it has been argued that this theory is inadequate because it fails to take into account the simplification of planning within a firm that monopoly makes possible. A monopolist must predict the behaviour of consumers and control his costs; but he does not have to fit his plans as best he may to those of competitors. The reduction of uncertainty may make capital projects attractive which would not be undertaken if full utilisation could not be assured.

Moreover, a monopoly may avoid wasteful duplication of capacity. In the late 1950's, for example, the British refrigerator industry invested in more capacity than the market warranted. This was one way of finding out which manufacturers were best fitted to make 'fridges. They are the ones who have survived. This competitive method of discovering the efficient use of resources has its attractions but it also has its costs.

Countervailing power. The planning advantage of monopoly has been seen by J. K. Galbraith as one of the foundations of the New

Industrial State. Galbraith is also associated with the notion of countervailing power, that one monopoly may be neutralised by selling to or buying from another. For instance, it is evident that the market power of manufacturers of heavy electrical equipment would not amount to much even if they acted together. At home they have only one customer, the Central Electricity Generating Board.

The presence of countervailing power is easily demonstrated. It is more difficult to show that there is any equality in the power of the two sides. In electricity the Generating Board could build its own equipment or buy from abroad. Equipment manufacturers are prevented by statute from entering the electricity supply industry, and they would have difficulty in selling abroad if their equipment was not acceptable to domestic users.

Terms of trade. The argument that a monopoly is desirable if it exploits foreigners is a despicable one, and, fortunately, there are few opportunities for it to be converted from a theoretical possibility to actuality. In most cases foreigners may buy from alternative suppliers in different countries. International trade is in fact one of the most obvious means for eroding monopoly power. Monopoly was a minor problem in Britain until free trade was abandoned in 1932.

Looking at the pros and cons of monopoly it can be seen that here is a condition which cannot be condemned outright but needs to be judged on its merits. The same has been said of the practice of resale price maintenance.

Resale price maintenance

This is the arrangement by which a manufacturer fixes not only the price at which he will sell at the factory gate but also the price at which his goods must be resold by retailers. In this way he determines the size of the gross margins for wholesaling and retailing. R.p.m. was introduced at the turn of the century when branded goods became important. Retailers exerted pressure through their trade associations to have r.p.m. adopted. In Britain the practice seems unlikely to survive the application of the Resale Prices Act, 1964.

The main undesirable features of r.p.m. are that it may

- raise prices and increase gross margins,
- increase the volume of resources devoted to retailing, and
- reduce the alternatives open to consumers.

On the other hand, r.p.m. may

- lead to a desirable increase in the facilities for retail distribution, or
- be a means of raising the volume of production and reducing costs where demand depends to a marked extent upon availability.

Wide margins and the extent of retailing. The presumption must be that r.p.m. makes retail prices higher and gross margins wider than they otherwise would be. If this were not so it would be difficult to explain why retailers have sought to have r.p.m. adopted. Wide margins are unlikely to be of permanent benefit to retailers as abnormal profits attract new entrants and impel existing retailers into providing better services, e.g. improved premises, a wider assortment of goods, free delivery or credit. There may be too many shops operating on too small a scale or too much service. In either case the volume of resources devoted to retailing is larger than would be the case with free price competition.

Opportunities closed. At the same time the number of alternatives available to consumers is reduced. An efficient retailer, providing the same services as his competitors at lower cost, cannot undercut their prices in order to expand, and so the pace of change in retailing is slowed down. A retailer offering fewer services cannot charge a correspondingly lower price. New or badly located retailers cannot give price incentives to gain patronage.

As one disadvantage is quoted after another r.p.m. seems a thoroughly undesirable arrangement. However, there are mitigating circumstances. It is possible that in some cases r.p.m. makes no material difference to prices and margins and so to retailing behaviour. It may simply be the institutional framework through which competitive forces operate. When r.p.m. does make a difference its effects might be beneficial.

Retail services. It is arguable that retail shops provide more than a means of getting goods to consumers, that they are also part of our way of life. We might be poorer for the absence of some shops which could not survive free price competition. This argument carried some weight with the Restrictive Practices Court when it judged that the Net Book Agreement, the arrangement for maintaining the prices of books, is in the public interest. Towns were thought to be culturally enriched by the presence of a bookshop. Chemists and publicans put forward similar claims.

Availability and demand. It was further argued in the case of books that the availability of literature on the shelves of stock-holding book-sellers increases the demand for books. This enables some titles to be published that would not otherwise be profitable, and other titles to be published in larger prints at lower wholesale prices and consequently lower retail prices. Availability influences demand for other commodities. For example, the temperance argument for limiting the opening hours of public houses is based on this demand relationship. When there are economies of scale in production, wide distribution attained by r.p.m. could be a means to lower costs and prices.

Monopoly profits

Monopoly profits represent a redistribution of income from consumers to shareholders. As ownership of ordinary shares is seldom a criterion of need or desert this redistribution is difficult to defend. Furthermore, monopoly profits are in a sense paid for not producing instead of producing. They are therefore disfunctional as well as inequitable. There is little difficulty in weighing pros and cons of monopoly profits; but there is difficulty in identifying such profits.

Monopoly profits are an economic concept. It is thus necessary to distinguish economic profit from accounting profit. When the economic profit has been discovered, further distinctions need to be made as economic profit may accrue for other reasons than monopoly.

Economic vs. accounting profit. Accounting profit differs from economic profit in two main respects.

- Accountants do not take account of all the costs incurred by enterprise owners before they strike the figure for profits.
- In inflationary times, accountants may deduct too little for depreciation before calculating profits.

Imputed costs. Economists argue that all alternatives foregone to enable production to be undertaken should be valued and added together to find total costs. When these are deducted from total receipts the economic profit is discovered. Accountants do not treat in this way resources supplied directly by the owners. In particular they do not impute a cost of capital supplied by ordinary and preference shareholders. Accounting profit therefore exceeds economic profit by the interest to be imputed on owners' capital.

Depreciation. Economists view depreciation as the fall in the value of fixed assets between the beginning and the end of an accounting year. At the beginning of the year, one can look forward to a stream of net receipts accruing from the use of the capital. The present value of this stream is the value of the capital. At the end of the year, part of the stream of net receipts will have been enjoyed or missed for ever and, looking forward once more, a new present value can be calculated. The difference between the present value of fixed assets at the beginning and end of the year is depreciation as seen by the economist.

At any time the market price of capital equipment should equal its present value so that, if prices remain constant, the accounting practice of deducting a proportion of the historical cost of equipment each year should approximate to economic depreciation. When prices are rising, however, the accounting conventions will underestimate the decline in the worth of equipment. Furthermore, the accountant will underestimate the worth of the equipment from which the decline occurs.

In inflationary times accounting profit exceeds economic profit because accountants may prefer to allow for the changing price level by a special reserve provision after they have calculated a profit figure. When profit is expressed as a ratio to capital employed the accounting figure is further ahead of the economic one because of the understatement of capital employed. For example, the ratio of I.C.I.'s accounting profit on fertilisers to capital employed, valued at historical cost, was 17·5 per cent in 1956/7. When the capital is revalued on a replacement cost basis the figure falls to 11·1 per cent. If we deduct 5 per cent as interest on the capital provided by shareholders we reach an economic profit of 6·1 per cent.

Sources of economic profit. Economic profit may accrue as

- windfalls,
- rewards for risk-taking, and
- rewards for innovation.

If none of these explanations is adequate, the profit may be attributed to monopoly.

Windfalls. Profits and losses occur because future demands and costs are estimated wrongly, or because adjustments to foreseen events lag behind. For example, the closure of the Suez Canal in 1967 presented windfall profits to tanker-owners and windfall losses to oil companies dependent on Middle East sources of crude oil. Windfalls are by their nature sporadic. Profit figures over a run of years are needed so that windfall elements can be identified.

Rewards for risk. The owners of business enterprises put their capital at hazard. It is to be expected that financial investors will restrict investment relative to demand to such levels that risk rewards earned by successful investors are sufficient to offset the losses of unsuccessful. This element has to be allowed for by looking at profits over the years of all suppliers in a market, or, when there is only one supplier, at a run of his profits. If a firm never makes losses, then the argument that risk-taking is being rewarded looks somewhat thin.

Innovation. The reward for being first with a new method or product is easier to identify because the method or product may be specified. As few firms innovate continuously one would not usually expect profits for innovation to be regularly earned.

When economic profit is distinguished from accounting profit and allowance made for windfalls, risk-taking and innovation, the amount of profit that can be attributed to monopoly is often modest. I.C.I. comment on their fertiliser profits: "The fertiliser nitrogen business is more hazardous than the average heavy manufacturing industry in this country, calling for a large investment in physical assets, with working capital likely to be tied up for long periods. The company submits that if the fertiliser business stood on its own, the new subscriber would expect a return of 7 to 10 per cent on his subscribed capital, plus an undistributed margin, making at least 15 per cent in all."[1]

Summary

● The presence of monopoly causes concern because it may lead to lethargic inefficiency, misallocation of resources, excess profits, and political intervention.

● On the other hand, it may provide means and scope for innovation, enable resources to be used by better-informed

[1] The Monopolies Commission, *Report on the Supply of Chemical Fertilisers*, London, H.M.S.O., 1959, p. 172.

managers, and provide its own antidote by the creation of points of countervailing power.

- R.p.m. is thought to raise prices, create excess capacity in retailing, and reduce the number of alternatives open to consumers.
- Large capacity in retailing may be welcomed at times because the shops contribute to culture or convenience, or because they create demand by making goods readily available.
- Monopoly profit is an element which may be sometimes found in economic profit. The latter differs from accounting profit by imputing costs to resources provided by enterprise-owners, and, in inflationary times, by treatment of depreciation on a replacement cost basis.
- Monopoly profit is the part of economic profit that cannot be attributed to windfalls, risk-taking or innovation.

Reading

J. A. Schumpeter, *Capitalism, Socialism and Democracy*, London, 1947.

J. K. Galbraith, *The New Industrial State*, London, 1967.

B. S. Yamey (ed.), *Resale Price Maintenance*, London, 1966.

J. S. Bain, *Industrial Organisation*, New York, 1959.

Chapter 9

THE CONTROL OF MONOPOLY

THE last two chapters have demonstrated the need to judge monopolistic arrangements on their merits. They may be for or against the public interest and one can only decide which by investigating them. This pragmatism has been characteristic of the British approach to the control of monopoly. It contrasts with American attitudes which are apt to regard competition as a way of life desirable for its own sake.

Another characteristic of British control has been reliance on publicity. It is believed that increasing information about the operation and effects of monopoly will lead to voluntary reform. This sometimes provokes cynicism, but it should be recognised that stereotypes of big business have been transformed in this century. At one time the talk was of "robber barons". Feudal metaphors are still favoured, but now the complaint is often made that large companies are too conscious of *noblesse oblige*, too given to "soulful" behaviour. Publicity has played some part in the transformation.

The main stages in British policy may be seen in a calendar of events.

1948: the Monopolies and Restrictive Practices Commission established.

1953: the Commission increased in size and authorised to sit in sub-groups.

1956: the Registrar of Restrictive Practices and Restrictive Practices Court established to deal with monopolistic agreements between firms. The Monopolies Commission reduced in size and limited to investigating dominant firm monopolies, export agreements and general practices. Collective resale price maintenance outlawed.

1964: individual r.p.m. to be registered and each case examined by the Restrictive Practices Court.

1965: the Monopolies Commission increased in size and given added powers to investigate large mergers and restrictive agreements in service trades.

In the first section the nature and operations of the Monopolies Commission are described and assessed. The second section is devoted to the Restrictive Practices Act 1956, and the third to the Restrictive Practices Court.

The Monopolies Commission

The Commission may be explained in the answers to four questions. What is it? Who is it? What does it do? How are its recommendations enforced? We are then in a position to review criticism of the Commission.

What is it? The Commission is an advisory committee reporting to the President of the Board of Trade. The President may refer a variety of subjects. (i) Dominant firm monopolies, i.e. firms supplying or processing more than one-third of the output of a good or service. Thus Imperial Tobacco for cigarettes, Unilever and Proctor and Gamble for synthetic detergents, and I.C.I. and Fisons for chemical fertilisers all came within the purview of the Commission. (ii) Restrictive agreements relating to exports between firms together controlling more than one-third of supplies of a good. The Commission rather than the Court is empowered to investigate such agreements because there might be need to keep matters confidential; but no such reference has been made. (iii) Restrictive agreements relating to the supply of services by people and firms providing more than one-third of a particular service: e.g. the "green cards agreement" on terms for insuring motorists touring abroad. (iv) Newspaper mergers where total circulations of more than 3 million copies are involved and none of the newspapers amalgamating is failing. Newspapers are subject to special treatment because of the danger to freedom of the press inherent in concentration of control. (v) Other mergers where amalgamation would create or strengthen a monopoly position or would involve more than £5 million assets. (vi) General practices: e.g. the practice of recommending resale prices has been referred to the Commission.

The Commission cannot institute any enquiries itself. It must await reference to it, when it may be asked to report on the facts or, as is generally the case, on the facts plus its analysis of the effects on the public interest.

It is sometimes suggested that the Commission should have power to undertake investigations on its own initiative; but it is difficult to see how an advisory committee can be left to decide for itself what it shall advise on. The suggestion may arise from suspicion that the Board of Trade might suppress embarrassing enquiries. This would not be easy to achieve. Anyone may complain to the Board of Trade about monopolies, and the list of complaints is published in an Annual Report. Questions in the House of Commons could be very embarrassing if anything was being wilfully suppressed.

Who is it? Commissioners are appointed by the President of the Board of Trade to serve for periods of from three to seven years. They cannot be reappointed for more than twelve years. The chairman is full-time and the others are part-time.

Commissioners have to act as investigators, prosecutors, defence counsel, judge and jury, so they need to be men of many talents. The public interest has not been defined by Parliament so the Commission has to decide what it is for itself. For this purpose it needs to be representative of the public as a whole, and this leads to a part-time, amateur Commission. The first Commission consisted of two seconded civil servants, two academic economists, two industrialists, two barristers, one trade union official and one accountant. Commissions have continued to be composed of these kinds of people.

Seen in the flesh the Commission is a group of middle-aged gentlemen, eminent in their full-time callings, who devote large parts of their time to this side-line activity. They are impressive, but not so formidable as the blue books they prepare. Presidents of the Board of Trade are sometimes criticised for not accepting the recommendations of the Commission. There is always the possibility that the Commission may be wrong.

What does it do? The Commission has the powers to secure evidence of a Royal Commission. Its first task is to establish the facts of production and supply in order to determine whether the conditions of the Acts apply. It does this mainly by questionnaires.

The Commission then proceeds to investigate effects of the monopoly on the public interest. Accountants examine costs and profits; but the accounting picture is often blurred because only part of the activities of a multi-product firm may be subject to a particular reference. Complaints are invited from the monopolist's suppliers, customers and competitors. Firms under investigation are faced with further questionnaires which seek to determine the effects of their operations.

From the point of view of the firms this stage is the most uncomfortable. They cannot be sure what the Commission is getting at when it asks open-ended questions. When questions are based on complaints the complainants are often kept anonymous, there is no opportunity to cross-examine them and reliance has to be placed on the Commission checking how genuine they are.

The enquiry on paper is followed by hearings in private. Companies are generally represented by Q.C.s, but this part of the procedure may seem something of a formality. Companies are under investigation. They do not have the opportunity to argue that the Commission's views on the public interest are mistaken. These views are in process of being formed, and only appear in the report.

Enforcement. When the Commission reports to the President of the Board of Trade, any recommendation it makes could be enforced by Order laid before Parliament. This procedure was adopted with the dental goods and timber references and attempted in the case of the Total Oil Company for petrol supply; but the Board of Trade prefers to secure compliance by obtaining informal undertakings from firms. This may augment the power of the ministry, and it avoids legal problems of drafting Orders and the danger that investigations may be repeated before judges by appeal on the legality of Orders. Firms probably prefer informality because they can exert influence, and informal undertakings are more easily modified than parliamentary Orders.

Criticisms. To the outsider the Commission is apt to appear another example of the British cult of the amateur. This may be inevitable for the Commission because of the need for a representative body capable of assessing the public interest; but it is not inevitable that the Commission be served, as at present, by a small group of general civil servants. It is sometimes suggested that the main work of investigation should be undertaken by permanent officials who would report to the Commission. However, investigation has to be guided by what is considered the public interest, so investigation and evaluation may be inseparable.

A second criticism is that the Commission is slow-working, taking up to five years to produce a report. This results to some extent from Commissioners being part-time, but it is also connected with the thoroughness of investigations. Monopoly problems are seldom such that there would be any gain from snap judgements.

Firms under investigation may find the Commission reminiscent of the Star Chamber. They probably think that they have been hauled before the Commission for no better reason than their business success to be judged with no proper opportunity to defend themselves. Views like these led businessmen to support the establishment of the Restrictive Practices Court where agreements could be openly attacked and defended and judgement reached by men carrying the prestige of judicial office.

The Restrictive Practices Act, 1956

Under the 1956 Act all restrictive agreements between firms, except export agreements, on such matters as prices, output and terms of trading must be registered with the Registrar of Restrictive Agreements. The register is open to inspection by the public. The Registrar must bring each agreement before the Restrictive Practices Court, which must declare agreements void if they do not satisfy one of six particular conditions and one general condition. An agreement cannot continue on the ground that it does no harm: it must be thought to be of some particular benefit.

The conditions are laid down in the six "gateways" and "tailpiece" of Section 21(1). The gateways form three groups of two:

- two are concerned with the protection and benefit of consumers;
- two deal with countervailing power; and
- two are concerned with general policy towards employment and exports.

Protection against injury. Subsection (a) reads that the Court may accept an agreement if it is satisfied that "the restriction is reasonably necessary, having regard to the character of the goods to which it applies, to protect the public against injury (whether to persons or to premises) in connection with the consumption, installation or use of those goods". The need to protect the public against injury was pleaded unsuccessfully by chemists with regard to trading in medicines, and by tyre traders with regard to fitting car tyres.

Subsection (a), seeking to take advantage of monopolistic arrangements in order to provide for public safety, is a legal curiosity. If there is need to protect the public, special legislation, such as that regarding electrical safety, would seem more appropriate.

Specific and substantial benefit. The gateway pleaded most often is "that the removal of the restriction would deny to the public as purchasers, consumers or users of any goods other specific and substantial benefits or advantages enjoyed or likely to be enjoyed by them as such, whether by virtue of the restriction itself or of any arrangements or operations resulting therefrom". This may seem a very wide gateway, but it should be noticed that benefits must be specific (a vague possibility will not do) and substantial (a little benefit is not enough).

This gateway has been negotiated by a number of agreements, and the successes have sometimes been surprising. The agreement on black bolts and nuts was accepted because it protected customers from the opportunity and expense of shopping around for lower prices. The cement makers agreement was thought to keep prices down because it was thought to reduce uncertainty and so enable investment to be undertaken at lower rates of interest. The agreement between manufacturers of permanent magnets was associated with the sharing of research results, and that of manufacturers of standard metal windows with technical co-operation. Price agreement between glazed and floor tile manufacturers enabled them to resist the temptation to introduce non-standard tiles at enhanced costs. The steel scrap agreement was accepted because it lowered the price of scrap, which was seen as a benefit to the users of scrap although evidently an equal detriment to the sellers of scrap.

Counter a dominant competitor. Subsection (c) reads that an agreement may be accepted if "the restriction is reasonably necessary to counteract measures taken by any one person not party to the agreement with a view to preventing or restricting competition in or in relation to the trade or business in which the persons party thereto are engaged". This gateway has not so far been pleaded.

Countervailing power. Subsection (d) allows a restriction to be accepted if it "is reasonably necessary to enable the persons party to the agreement to negotiate fair terms for the supply of goods to, or the acquisition of goods from, any one person not party thereto who controls a preponderant part of the trade or business of acquiring or supplying such goods, or for the supply of goods to any person not party to the agreement and not carrying on such trade or business who, either alone or in combination with any other such person, controls a preponderant part of the market for such goods". This gateway was passed by the sulphuric acid manufacturers, who argued that their agreement was necessary to enable them to face up to large foreign suppliers of sulphur.

Local unemployment. The last two gateways symbolise national neurosis regarding unemployment and exports. Monopolistic agreements are not to be condemned if it can be shown that "having regard to the conditions actually obtaining or reasonably foreseen at the time of the application, the removal of the restriction would be likely to have a serious and persistent adverse effect upon the general level of unemployment in an area, or in areas taken together, in which a substantial proportion of the trade or industry to which the agreement relates is situated".

Cartels may engage in work-spreading and so provide intermittent employment for many rather than continuous employment for a smaller number; but their most likely effect is to reduce the total amount of employment they offer. The preservation of monopoly is a bizarre way of attempting to deal with the general level of employment, which is best tackled by budgetary and monetary policies. Localised unemployment calls for regional policies and not cartellisation. The yarn spinners passed this gateway before being caught by the "tailpiece". The arguments on which the judges reached their decision on the gateway were subsequently proved wrong by events in Lancashire.

Exports. The export gateway is even more of an economic nonsense. A restrictive agreement may be accepted if it can be shown that "having regard to the conditions actually obtaining or reasonably foreseen at the time of the application, the removal of the restriction would be likely to cause a reduction in the volume or earnings of the export business which is substantial either in relation to the whole export business of the United Kingdom or in relation to the whole business (including export business) of the said trade or industry".

This clause is a monument to the powers of survival of mercantalist fallacies. There is the unworthy germ of truth in the clause that a national monopoly may be able to exploit foreigners; but it is doubtful whether the legislators had this in mind. Concern over the volume of exports is misplaced, and earnings only matter in relation to overseas expenditures. The balance of payments as a whole, rather than exports alone, is the subject for concern. On the export side, it is the absolute money value of exports which matters and not whether this is substantial relative to the whole business of a particular industry. Restrictive agreements are not efficient means for dealing with balance of payments problems. This gateway was successfully pleaded by the makers of water-tube boilers, who argued that their agreement enabled them to gain export orders by facilitating the exchange of technical and commercial information about foreign requirements by ensuring that the keenest price was quoted by the supplier enjoying the goodwill of the foreign customer, and by enabling sales offices to be maintained abroad.

The tailpiece. If an agreement is found to pass one or other of the gateways, the Court has to weigh the particular benefit against any general detriments. The tailpiece of Section 21(1) reads that, when the Court decides that favourable circumstances justify a restriction, it must be further satisfied that "the restriction is not unreasonable having regard to the balance between those circumstances and any detriment to the public or to persons not parties to the agreement (being purchasers, consumers or users of goods produced or sold by such parties, or persons engaged or seeking to become engaged in the trade or business of selling such goods or of producing or selling similar goods) resulting or likely to result from the operation of the restriction". In the yarn spinners' case, when the pros and cons were balanced overall it was decided that the agreement was against the public interest because it maintained too large a labour force, increased prices and harmed exports.

The Restrictive Practices Court

A special court, of High Court status, was set up by the 1956 Act. At least one high court judge and two lay judges sit together to hear cases. It is to be expected that the judge with the full legal background will carry the greatest influence.

Some of the contradictions to be found in judgements may stem from the three judges arguing in opposite senses. There are no dissenting judgements or indications of disagreement. Evidence is submitted in writing in advance of oral proceedings. Representatives of the associates in a restrictive agreement plead that the agreement should pass particular gateways. The Registrar of Restrictive Trading Agreements pleads the detriments.

Establishing gateways. The task of the lawyers defending a restrictive agreement is made difficult by the tight wording of the Act. It is easy to think that an Act of Parliament means what one thinks M.P.s intended. In a court of law it is the actual words that matter. For example, the Act implies that harmless agreements are to be condemned.

Establishing detriments. The Registrar's task of showing that an agreement is against the public interest is easy for detrimental things that parties to the agreement have done. For example, when the Scottish bakers decided not to reduce the price of bread when the cost of materials fell, or when bottle manufacturers refused to supply lightweight beer bottles for filling with vinegar, they did something which left a record which could be quoted and analysed. It is more difficult for the Registrar to establish that detriment has occurred because some things have not been done: costs have not been reduced, technological advances have not been made, or managerial enterprise has not been exerted. This same problem has to be faced in another form by the judges.

Problems of judgement. The difficulty of judging a restrictive agreement lies in the fact that judges are called upon to compare two hypothetical situations: what might be without the agreement with what might be with the agreement. Knowledge of what has been with the agreement in the past is at best only of limited relevance.

It can be persuasively argued that the desirability of a restrictive agreement is not a justiciable question. The public interest is a political matter and should not be left to be defined by judges weighing detriments against benefits in the light of the questionable and imprecise criteria of the 1956 Act.

Effects. A restrictive agreement which would fail to pass the Court may be superseded by firms merging and so converting the agreement into an internal policy of the combine. Mergers of significant size, however, are subject to investigation by the Monopolies Commission. A price agreement may be replaced by the practice of rivals keeping each other continuously informed about prices charged so that they may arrive at an agreed price level by implicit agreement. Again a price agreement may be replaced by one associate becoming price-leader and the rest price-followers. The 1956 Act can thus be avoided; but the 2110 agreements abandoned between 1956 and 1966 were not all replaced by one or other of these devices. Business attitudes have been modified. It is now respectable to compete.

Looking at industry one cannot help but be aware of change and growth. This is partly the result of the economies of scale, organisational developments, research and development, and technological innovation examined in Part One. It is also a consequence of the changed climate of opinion that the Monopolies Commission and Restrictive Practices Court have helped to create.

Summary

- The British approach to the control of monopoly has been pragmatic and has relied to a considerable extent on publicity for securing improvement.

- The Monopolies Commission is a part-time advisory committee empowered to investigate dominant firm monopolies and mergers referred to it by the President of the Board of Trade.
- It is amateur, slow moving and inquisitorial, or, in other words, it is representative, thorough and holds the powers of a Royal Commission.
- Restrictive agreements can only survive the 1956 Act if they can be shown to protect consumers, provide specific and substantial benefit, confer countervailing power, preserve employment or increase exports. If an agreement passes one of these gateways it still has to be weighed in the light of the public interest as a whole.
- Showing in the Restrictive Practices Court that an agreement deserves to pass one of the gateways is difficult because of the tight wording of the Act.
- Establishing detriments is easy for things done, but difficult for things left undone.
- It is doubtful whether these matters are justiciable. Judges are called upon to make economic predictions, and then to act in a quasi-political capacity whilst deciding the public interest.
- The 1956 Act may be avoided by merger, open price-exchange agreements and price leadership; but many agreements have been abandoned and the industrial climate has become more bracing.

Reading

R. B. Stevens and B. S. Yamey, *The Restrictive Practices Court*, London, 1965.

Oxford Economic Papers, November 1965.

Monopolies Commission Reports.

INDEX